EVERYONE**CAN**COOK
slow cooker meals

ERIC AKIS

EVERYONE**CAN**COOK
slow cooker meals

recipes for satisfying mains
and delicious sides

whitecap

Whitecap Books is known for its expertise in the
cookbook market, and has produced some of
the most innovative and familiar titles found in
kitchens across North America. Visit our website
at www.whitecap.ca.

Edited by Lesley Cameron
Interior design by Michelle Furbacher and
    Jacqui Thomas
Food photography by Michael Tourigny
Food and prop styling by Eric Akis
Author photo by Tyler Akis

 Recipes in this book were tested
with an All-Clad slow cooker.

Printed in China by 1010 Printing Asia Ltd.

LIBRARY AND ARCHIVES CANADA CATALOGUING
IN PUBLICATION

Akis, Eric, 1961–
    Everyone can cook slow cooker meals : recipes
for satisfying mains and delicious sides / Eric Akis.

Includes index.
ISBN 978-1-77050-027-3

1. Electric cookery, Slow. I. Title.

TX827.A42 2010   641.5'884   C2010-903164-4

The publisher acknowledges the financial support
of the Government of Canada through the Canada
Book Fund (CBF) and the Province of British
Columbia through the Book Publishing Tax Credit.

11 12 13 14   5 4 3 2

EVERYONE**CAN**COOK
slow cooker meals

ACKNOWLEDGMENTS

Producing a cookbook is a mountain of work, but reaching the summit is easier when the author has talented people helping him along the way.

Some of those whom I must graciously thank can be found in the offices of Whitecap Books, where publisher Robert McCullough, editor Taryn Boyd, designer Michelle Furbacher and a host of others turn my work into something delicious to look at and to cook from. Before they do that, another person I must thank, freelance editor Lesley Cameron, reviews my words and collaborates with me to create a manuscript worth celebrating.

Of course, that manuscript contains only words; the stunning photographs you see in this book come later. Thank you to talented photographer Michael Tourigny for making my culinary ideas look so appealing.

I'd also like to thank All-Clad for supplying the slow cooker used to test these recipes. During the creation of this book, I used this slow cooker every day, sometimes twice a day, for about six months, and it performed admirably.

Finally, and most importantly, thanks to my wife, Cheryl, and son, Tyler, for standing by me, offering words of support and providing helpful suggestions on the book's content during the many months it took to produce. You are the best!

INTRODUCTION

If anyone had asked me ten years ago if I would ever publish a slow cooker cookbook, I would have responded, "Are you crazy?" I was a professionally trained chef and knowledgeable food writer and, at that time, the idea of throwing a bunch of things into a machine, pressing a button and cooking them all day was not my idea of "real" cooking.

Well, I'm still that same chef and food writer, but about five years ago my opinions about slow cookers did an about-face when my wife, who knew their value, came home with one, declaring she would be using it. I said quite emphatically that I would not, but not long after that, a company I develop recipes for, and readers of my newspaper column, started asking me for slow cooker recipes. It was almost like a conspiracy. This electrical appliance has been around since the 1970s and had fallen out of favor for some time, but of late it has become trendy again. With folks being so busy these days, having a meal ready in your slow cooker when you get home from work makes sense.

Reluctantly, I gave it a try. The first dish I made was beef chili. After it had cooked for eight hours in the slow cooker, I opened the lid and gave it a stir. Its aroma, look and taste were every bit as good as any chili I've made on the stovetop. I was a slow cooker convert!

Since that first experiment, I've successfully cooked all sorts of other dishes in it, many of which are in this book, such as Poached Fish in a Saffron, Orange and Fennel Broth (page 50) and Lamb Shanks Braised with Wine, Citrus and Spice (page 148).

Those two slow cooker dishes, and several others in this book, would certainly be suitable for a special occasion, while many other recipes are more for everyday dining, such as Chicken and Vegetable Stew (page 75), and Sweet-and-Sour Pork with Ginger and Pineapple (page 109). As well as meat, poultry and seafood recipes, this book includes slow cooker main course soups and vegetarian dishes.

There are numerous slow cooker cookbooks on the market, but I haven't come across one that also offers a tantalizing mix of dishes to serve alongside. You can cook a complete meal in a slow cooker, but quite often you'll find yourself cooking a main meal that needs a tasty side dish to complement it.

In this book, I provide a range of easy-to-make, delicious side dish recipes made on the stovetop, in the oven or in a bowl that will complement what you cooked in the slow cooker and take it to the next taste level.

For example, I suggest serving the Sake Soy Braised Beef Short Ribs (page 134) with Ginger Mashed Squash (page 209). This quickly cooked stovetop side dish has a stunning orange color and gingery taste that pairs perfectly with the dark and delicious ribs. For the Fall Vegetable and Bean Stew (page 31), I recommend serving a side dish that will tastily soak up its sauce, such as Rice Pilaf with Thyme, Lemon and Garlic (page 183).

I make these kinds of suggestions for the majority of the slow cooker main course recipes in this book. Some recipes, however, are pretty much a complete meal, and for those I simply suggest what could be served alongside to enhance the main course. For example, I suggest serving Pork Back Ribs in Sauerkraut (page 105), a German-style meal strewn with vegetables, with boiled potatoes, dill pickles and spicy mustard.

The book starts with a section called Slow Cooking 101 that explains how a slow cooker works and offers numerous tips on using it. For example, why do cooking times vary in some recipes? What do you do if the power goes out? It also explains that the recipes in this book were tested in and designed for slow cookers with a 4½- to 6½-quart (4.5 to 6.5 L) capacity.

As in the first five books in my bestselling Everyone Can Cook series, the recipes in this volume are designed for all levels of cooks and use ingredients found in most supermarkets. "Eric's Options," included with each recipe, offer suggestions for substituting some ingredients or adding others to bring the dish to another level.

With a copy of *Everyone Can Cook Slow Cooker Meals: Recipes for Satisfying Mains and Delicious Sides* in your kitchen, mealtimes will become a complete and very delicious experience.

SLOW COOKING 101

Before you start using the slow cooker recipes in this book, read this guide to learn more about the machine and how to make the most of it.

WHAT IS A SLOW COOKER?
Slow cookers consist of a metal container that holds a ceramic pot. Housed inside the walls of the container is a heating element that surrounds the pot, but does not touch it. This, and the thickness and heaviness of the pot, promotes even cooking and prevents foods from sticking and burning.

Once the food is in the pot and the lid is in place, you simply choose your setting, turn the machine on and let things start cooking. As the food cooks, steam builds up in the pot, rises and hits the top of the lid and falls back onto the food, keeping it moist and preventing it from drying out, even after many hours of cooking.

WHAT TYPE TO BUY?
If you don't already have a slow cooker, you should first consider what you'll use it for before you buy one. If it's simply to heat small portions of soup, make single portions of oatmeal or make a hot dip for a party, buy a small slow cooker with about a 1-quart (1 L) capacity.

However, if your goal is to prepare a diverse range of meals, where in some cases you'll want tasty leftovers that you can freeze and enjoy at another time, buy an oval-shaped slow cooker with a 4½- to 6½-quart (4.5 to 6.5 L) capacity. Those sizes are perfect for cooking four or more servings of food. The oval shape, which offers a wider cooking surface than a round slow cooker, also gives you greater flexibility in what you can cook in it.

All the recipes in this book were tested in, and designed for, slow cookers with a 4½- to 6½-quart (4.5 to 6.5 L) capacity.

Slow cookers are all fairly similar in how they work, but before you begin using your new slow cooker, read the manual thoroughly to determine if there are any special guidelines on using that particular model beyond the tips noted here.

ABOUT THE SETTINGS

As the food warms in the pot it rises to a food-safe cooking temperature—
that is, between approximately 185°F and 280°F (85°C to 138°C), depending on
the setting.

The low setting, logically, cooks foods at a lower temperature and more slowly
than the high setting. Most recipes in this book call for the low setting, as people
tend to use slow cookers so they can have a meal simmering away when they
return home, hours later, from a busy day. The low setting also cooks food,
whether cubes of meat or chunks of vegetables, more gently, ensuring it holds
together even after hours of cooking.

The high setting is for times when you want the food cooked more quickly, and
that setting can be used for the recipes in this book. One hour of cooking on the
high setting is equivalent to about 2 hours on the low setting. So, for example, if
a recipe requires 8 hours on the low setting, it will require only about 4 hours on
the high setting. Also, if you started a recipe on the low setting and you are ready
to eat but the food is not, you could turn the slow cooker to high to speed up the
cooking. Or, if a dish takes 5 hours to cook on low, and you have only 4 hours,
you could give the dish a head start by setting the slow cooker to high for an hour
and then turning it to low for 3 hours.

Some slow cookers also have a medium setting that will cook food at a
temperature somewhere between that of the low and high settings. Most modern
machines will also have a warming mode that will keep the finished dish at a
food-safe temperature until you are ready to eat it, which is very useful if the dish
will have finished cooking before you return home.

BE ORGANIZED

If you want to get something slow-cooking first thing in the morning, do some
preparation the night before, such as chopping vegetables and measuring liquid
ingredients. Store everything in the refrigerator until you are ready to add it to
your slow cooker.

DON'T OVERFILL

If you fill a slow cooker too close to the rim it will take the food forever to start simmering and cooking. It will also be unsafe. If the machine gets bumped when it is too full, hot liquid may spill over the sides. It's best to fill a slow cooker no more than half to two-thirds full.

CHECKING FOR DONENESS

With any kind of cooking, whether you are roasting a chicken in the oven or steaming vegetables on the stovetop, it's difficult to resist opening the oven door or pot lid to see how things are progressing. With a slow cooker, though, you should only do that near or at the end of the first recommended cooking time. If you remove the lid, particularly early on in the cooking process, it can take 15 to 20 minutes or even more to return to the proper cooking temperature, which in turn means the food will take longer to cook.

When you do remove the lid, lift it almost straight up, with the lid tipped only very slightly up on the side opposite to you. This will ensure that hot steam from the slow cooker does not rise toward you and that any moisture on the lid does not drip into the slow cooker, potentially diluting the flavor of the food.

COOKING TIMES

In this book and other slow cooker cookbooks, you'll often see a range of cooking times given in recipes, such as 6 to 8 hours for a meaty stew. This is because the temperature the food cooks at can range from slow cooker to slow cooker, with newer, more efficient machines often cooking more quickly than older models. Household voltages can also vary and this too can affect cooking times.

In addition to the *Slow cooker time*, you'll see *Preparation time* and *Finishing time* listed at the top of each recipe. *Preparation time* is the approximate time spent getting the ingredients ready before you hit the On button. *Slow cooker time* is the main cooking time—how long you can walk away after turning on your slow cooker (although sometimes I will get you to boil pasta, prepare croutons, etc. during this time). For those recipes where you have to add ingredients to the slow cooker after the main cooking time, this is included in the *Finishing time*.

For example, for the salmon chowder (page 4), the main slow cooker time is 6 hours for the stock and vegetables. You then finish the chowder by adding the salmon and cream and letting it cook for 10 minutes more, during which you're chopping up the green onions for the garnish.

TO BROWN OR NOT TO BROWN

Some people like the idea of a slow cooker because they believe all you need to do to make a meal is throw everything into it, turn it on and walk away. That is certainly the case in some circumstances, including some of the tasty meat recipes in this book. For example, in the recipe for Sweet-and-Sour Pork with Ginger and Pineapple (page 109), I don't feel the need to brown the pork as the saucy ingredients in which the pork is cooked give the raw cubes of meat a rich color and flavor. In other dishes, though—Beef Daube (page 122), for example— it's very worthwhile to take the time to brown the meat. It can richly enhance its color and flavor and that of the other ingredients it is slow-cooked with.

Ground meat, such as beef or turkey, should always be browned first to enhance their color and to enable you to drain away any excess fat before adding them to the slow cooker.

Do not brown meat in your slow cooker insert unless yours is one designed for use on the stovetop.

FROZEN FOODS

Don't put frozen meat in a slow cooker; always thaw it first. Frozen meat will take too long to cook and could simmer at an unsafe temperature while doing so. Small frozen vegetables, such as peas, can be added near the end of cooking. They won't take long to heat through and will maintain their bright color.

SIZE MATTERS

It is important to cut the ingredients as called for in the recipe. If you're asked to cut a piece of beef into 1-inch (2.5 cm) cubes and you make the cubes twice that size, they'll take much longer to cook and your dish won't meet its target cooking time. The same goes for vegetables. In this book, I'll ask you to mince garlic, which means to finely chop. I also ask you to dice, which means to cut into

¼-inch (6 mm) cubes. Sometimes I simply ask you to cube a vegetable or piece of meat, and unless I give a specific size, that means ½-inch (1 cm) cubes.

THICKENING SAUCES

Some slow cooker recipes ask you to thicken a recipe, such as a stew, by pushing the food to one side of the pot and mixing a mixture of flour and water or a flavored liquid, called a slurry, into the sauce. You then turn the heat to high and simmer until it is thickened.

I did not use that technique in this book. It is rather awkward to push food, such as a dense mix of tender meat or vegetables, to one side of the pot. You could potentially break it apart while doing so. I also find it difficult to lose that uncooked flour taste unless I simmer the food for quite some time after mixing in the slurry, which can put dinner on hold for a while.

When using flour as a thickener, I opted to add it at the beginning of cooking. I do this in three ways. In some recipes I coated the meat with flour, browned it and added it to the slow cooker. In other recipes I thickened a sauce with flour on the stovetop before adding it to the slow cooker. Lastly, in some cases, at the start of cooking, I simply blended the flour into the liquid ingredients in the slow cooker, before adding the solid ingredients. All these approaches worked well.

WHAT IF THE FOOD COOKS FOR LONGER THAN SUGGESTED?

Foods can certainly overcook in a slow cooker. However, most recipes cooked on the low setting cook so slowly that they will not turn into an overcooked mush if you exceed the suggested cooking time by an hour or so, and will hold well if you have a warming mode.

WHAT IF THE POWER GOES OUT?

If you return home and the power is out, you'll have to decide what to do with the food in your slow cooker. If you insert an instant-read thermometer into the contents of the slow cooker and it's above the bacteria-killing temperature of 140°F (60°C), you can finish off the cooking in a pot on the stovetop or gas grill. However, if the food is between 40°F (4°C) and 140°F (60°C)—what health authorities call the danger zone in which bacteria can rapidly develop—you should throw the food out.

READ THE RECIPE

To ensure you have all the ingredients that you need, and that you have set aside enough time to prepare them, always read the recipe you wish to make a couple times before you begin.

FREEZING LEFTOVERS

If you have any leftovers from a recipe in this book, you can freeze them. To do so quickly and safely, remove the food from the slow cooker and set it in a bowl. Set the bowl in the sink and surround it with a mix of ice and cold water to a level that matches the level of the food in the bowl. Cool the food to room temperature, stirring it gently every so often. Pack the food into freezer containers in portion sizes that best meet your needs. Label and date and, for the best quality, use within two months of freezing. Thaw the food in the refrigerator the night before you intend to reheat it.

ADAPTING CONVENTIONAL RECIPES FOR A SLOW COOKER

If you have a favorite old recipe, or a new one that you absolutely must try, that's cooked in the oven or on the stovetop, you could adapt it for cooking in your slow cooker. The recipes best suited to being adapted are those that are simmered—such as soups, stews, curries and chili—and braised dishes, which, logically, do well in the moist cooking environs of a slow cooker.

Because of the moist cooking environment, where steam rises from the food, hits the lid and drips back on the food, the dish you are cooking can actually increase in volume as it cooks. Therefore, an important step in adapting a recipe for a slow cooker is to reduce the amount of liquids—such as stock or tomato sauce—you add. However, I first make the recipe using the ingredient amounts as listed. I'll then sample the dish and, if I find it much thinner than the original, I'll cut back on the liquid the next time I prepare it by a quarter, a third or even a half, depending on its consistency. It may take a few tries to get the recipe exactly where you want it, but your taste buds will thank you for your effort.

While you may need to reduce the amount of liquid in some recipes, you may need to increase the amount of flavorings you add to others as long, slow cooking can diminish the potency of some flavorings. So, for example, if a recipe calls for 1 clove of garlic, or 1 tsp (5 mL) of hot sauce, you may want to double or even triple that amount depending on your tastes.

Another important step in adapting recipes for a slow cooker is in how you cut the food. For example, if you have a stew recipe that says to add large chunks of potatoes or other root vegetables, you'll now need to cut them into smaller cubes, no more than 1 inch (2.5 cm) in size. If you don't, those large chunks might not be cooked through, even after many hours in a slow cooker.

If a recipe asks you to stir in a dairy product, such as light cream, do so at the very end of cooking. It may separate if simmered for an extended period of time in your slow cooker.

When you're wondering how long to cook a conventional recipe in a slow cooker, flip through the pages of this book. You'll find a wide range of dishes that will guide you.

CLEANING A SLOW COOKER
Let the insert of the slow cooker cool down before cleaning. It is sensitive to rapid heat changes and could be damaged if you are not careful. Also, do not fill the metal insert with water. Instead, once it's cooled down, wipe it clean and refer to the manual for detailed cleaning and maintenance information.

SATISFYING MAINS

MAIN COURSE SOUPS

CREAMY SEAFOOD CHOWDER
with CLAMS, SHRIMP and CRAB

Three of my favorite types of seafood are combined in this deluxe version of chowder infused with the smoky taste of bacon. This makes a fine and filling lunch or dinner when served with Buttermilk Biscuits (page 156).

preparation time	•	20 minutes
slow cooker time	•	6 hours
finishing time	•	15 minutes
makes	•	8 servings

6 thick slices bacon, diced

Three 10 oz (284 mL) cans clam nectar or juice

¼ cup (60 mL) all-purpose flour

1 lb (500 g) russet or Yukon Gold potatoes, peeled and cut into ¼-inch (6 mm) cubes

10 oz (284 mL) can baby clams

1 medium onion, diced

1 medium carrot, diced

1 large celery stalk, diced

1 garlic clove, minced

1 tsp (5 mL) dried thyme

½ lb (250 g) cooked salad shrimp

4 oz (125 g) can crabmeat, with leg and body meat drained well

1¼ cups (310 mL) light (10%) cream

Salt and white pepper to taste

2 Tbsp (30 mL) chopped fresh parsley

ERIC'S OPTIONS

Clam nectar and clam juice are the liquids produced after clams have been processed. They're sold in cans and bottles and you'll find them in most supermarkets. They're great for chowder and other seafood soups and sauces. If you can't find them, you could use fish or even chicken stock in this recipe. If you still want to infuse the chowder with a smoky taste, but don't want to use bacon, add 3 oz (90 g) of cold- or hot-smoked salmon, finely chopped, to the chowder when stirring in the shrimp and crab.

Fry the bacon until crispy, then drain well. Place the clam nectar and flour in your slow cooker and whisk until the flour is fully dissolved. Mix in the bacon, potatoes, baby clams and their liquid, onion, carrot, celery, garlic and thyme.

Cover and cook on the low setting for 6 hours, or until the potatoes are tender. Stir in the shrimp, crabmeat and cream. Cover and cook until everything is heated through, about 15 minutes. Season the chowder with salt and pepper. Sprinkle servings of the chowder with chopped parsley.

ABOUT CHOWDER

Chowder is derived from the French word *chaudière*, which means cauldron. Early French settlers who fished off Canada's east coast used these pots on their boats to cook up some of the day's catch into a stew-like mixture that eventually became known as chowder.

It soon became popular on land as well, and was an ideal way to use up household staples. Some early versions were made by combining rendered salt pork with fish or shellfish in simmering water and thickening the mixture with biscuits or bread.

As the soup evolved, potatoes began to replace or supplement the biscuits or bread, milk and cream were used, and bacon was an occasional substitute for the salt pork. Other styles of chowder also began to appear, such as the tomato-based Manhattan chowder, named after the city it was invented in.

SALMON and CORN CHOWDER with TARRAGON

I was inspired to make this soup one September day when both wild salmon and corn were in season. They are both harvested not far from my home, and they go together quite naturally. The somewhat oily taste of the fish is nicely balanced by the sweetness of the corn. I like to serve this chowder with good-quality crackers, either store-bought or homemade (such as [pictured] Sea Salt and Olive Oil Crackers on page 162).

3½ cups (875 mL) chicken or fish stock

¼ cup (60 mL) all-purpose flour

2 medium red-skinned potatoes (unpeeled), cut in ¼-inch (6 mm) cubes

2 cups (500 mL) fresh or frozen corn kernels

1 medium onion, finely diced

1 large celery stalk, finely diced

1 garlic clove, minced

½ cup (125 mL) dry white wine

1 tsp (5 mL) dried tarragon

1 lb (500 g) salmon fillets, skin removed, flesh cut into small cubes

1 cup (250 mL) light (10%) cream

Salt and white pepper to taste

2 green onions, thinly sliced

preparation time	•	25 minutes
slow cooker time	•	6 hours
finishing time	•	10 minutes
makes	•	6 servings

ERIC'S OPTIONS

If you like the taste of fresh dill, use 2 to 3 tsp (10 to 15 mL) of it chopped instead of the dried tarragon. Stir it into the soup when mixing in the salmon. Instead of salmon, you could try another firm fish fillet in this recipe, such as halibut. The cooking time will remain the same.

Place the stock and flour in your slow cooker. Whisk until the flour is completely dissolved. Mix in the potatoes, corn, onion, celery, garlic, wine and tarragon. Cover and cook on the low setting for 6 hours, or until the vegetables are tender. Mix in the salmon and cream. Cover and cook for 10 minutes more, or until the salmon is cooked through. Season the chowder to taste with salt and pepper. Sprinkle servings with green onion.

VEGETABLE-RICH SOUP with WHITE BEANS

The seven vegetables and one legume make this soup taste good and look good, and make it good *for* you. I like to serve it with slices of warm baguette and pistou (see Eric's Options).

6 cups (1.5 L) chicken or vegetable stock

19 oz (540 mL) can white kidney beans, drained, rinsed in cold water and drained again

3 Tbsp (45 mL) tomato paste

1 cup (250 mL) fresh or frozen corn kernels

2 medium red-skinned potatoes (unpeeled), cubed

1 medium onion, diced

1 large carrot, sliced into ¼-inch (6 mm) thick coins

1 large celery stalk, halved lengthwise and sliced

2–3 garlic cloves, minced

1 tsp (5 mL) dried oregano

1 tsp (5 mL) dried thyme

1 bay leaf

2 cups (500 mL) loosely packed fresh spinach, chopped

Salt and freshly ground black pepper to taste

preparation time	•	20 minutes
slow cooker time	•	6 hours
finishing time	•	5 minutes
makes	•	8 servings

ERIC'S OPTIONS

I like to spoon some pistou, a nut-free, French-style pesto, into the soup just before devouring. It adds to the richness of the flavor. To make pistou, place 2 cups (500 mL) of loosely packed fresh basil leaves, 2 minced garlic cloves and ½ cup (125 mL) of freshly grated Parmesan cheese in a food processor and pulse until finely chopped. Pour in ¼ cup (60 mL) olive oil and pulse until it is well incorporated, adding a little more oil if you find the pistou too thick.

Combine the stock, beans, tomato paste, corn, potatoes, onion, carrot, celery, garlic, oregano, thyme and bay leaf in your slow cooker. Cover and cook on the low setting for 6 hours, or until the vegetables are tender. Mix in the spinach. Cover and cook the soup until the spinach just wilts, about 5 minutes more. Season with salt and pepper and serve.

ABOUT LEGUMES

Legume is the name given to a wide variety of plant species with edible seedpods that split along both sides when ripe. Some of the more familiar varieties are lentils, soybeans, kidney beans, black-eyed peas, black beans and lima beans.

Legumes are available canned and dried. Dried legumes can be soaked overnight in cold water to speed up the cooking by 10 to 15 minutes. The overnight soak can also help freshen the taste of some varieties, such as split peas. Dried legumes can also be cooked from their dried state; just be sure to use a generous amount of water as they will expand and absorb a lot of water as they cook.

The time-pressed will be pleased to know that legumes are also sold fully cooked and canned, making them a convenient ingredient to open and add to a wide variety of recipes, including several in this book.

I always rinse canned legumes in cold water before using to remove the often sodium-rich liquid they are canned in.

VEGETARIAN LENTIL SOUP
with HERBES de PROVENCE

This hearty, meatless soup (pictured on page 11) is not only easy to make, it's also nutritious thanks to the lentils, which contain protein, fiber, B vitamins and other good things. I like to serve this soup with slices of Rosemary Flatbread (page 161) for dunking.

3 cups (750 mL) vegetable stock

Two 19 oz (540 mL) cans lentils, drained, rinsed and drained again

14 oz (398 mL) can tomato sauce

2 celery stalks, quartered lengthwise and thinly sliced

2 garlic cloves, minced

1 medium onion, finely diced

1 large carrot, quartered lengthwise and thinly sliced

1½ tsp (7.5 mL) herbes de Provence (see Note)

Salt and freshly ground black pepper to taste

Chopped fresh parsley to taste

Combine the stock, lentils, tomato sauce, celery, garlic, onion, carrot and herbes de Provence in your slow cooker. Cover and cook on the low setting for 6 hours, or until the vegetables are tender. Season the soup with salt and pepper. Sprinkle servings with parsley.

preparation time	•	10 minutes
slow cooker time	•	6 hours
makes	•	6–8 servings

NOTE

Herbes de Provence is an aromatic, French-style herb blend sold in bottles or bags at most supermarkets and fine food stores. The types of herbs used vary from producer to producer, but some commonly used ones include marjoram, lavender, sage, rosemary, savory and thyme.

ERIC'S OPTIONS

If you are a meat-eater, you could use chicken stock instead of vegetable stock. You could also roast or grill and thinly slice two fresh chorizo sausages to add to the soup at the start of cooking.

SPICED YAM and RED PEPPER SOUP with YOGURT

This silky, aromatic soup is boldly flavored with cumin, coriander and cayenne pepper. I like to serve it with grilled wedges of pita or naan bread. Simply brush a pita or naan lightly with olive oil. Grill the bread over medium-high heat until hot and lightly charred, about 1 minute per side.

preparation time	• 20 minutes
slow cooker time	• 6 hours
finishing time	• 10 minutes
makes	• 6–8 servings

5½ cups (1.375 L) chicken or vegetable stock

½ cup (125 mL) orange juice

2 Tbsp (30 mL) all-purpose flour

2 lb (1 kg) yams, peeled and cubed

1 large red bell pepper, cubed

½ medium onion, halved and sliced

2 Tbsp (30 mL) peeled, chopped fresh ginger (See About Fresh Ginger on page 30)

2 garlic cloves, minced

2 tsp (10 mL) ground cumin

¾ tsp (4 mL) ground coriander

⅛ tsp (0.5 mL) cayenne pepper

Salt and white pepper to taste

½ cup (125 mL) full- or low-fat plain yogurt, or to taste

2 green onions, thinly sliced

ERIC'S OPTIONS
For another taste element and a crunchy texture, sprinkle bowls of the soup with toasted, sliced almonds. Simply place ⅓ cup (80 mL) of sliced almonds in a single layer in a small baking pan and bake at 325°F (160°C), stirring occasionally, for 10 to 15 minutes, or until lightly toasted.

Place the stock, orange juice and flour in your slow cooker and whisk until the flour is completely dissolved. Mix in the yams, bell pepper, onion, ginger, garlic, cumin, coriander and cayenne. Cover and cook on the low setting for 6 hours, or until the vegetables are very tender. Purée the contents of the slow cooker with an immersion blender. (You could also purée the soup in a food processor or blender.) Thin the soup with a bit more stock if you find it too thick. Cover and cook for 10 minutes more, or until the soup is piping hot. Season with salt and white pepper. Top bowls of the soup with a dollop of yogurt and a sprinkling of green onion.

ROOT VEGETABLE SOUP
with BLUE CHEESE

Fairly plain tasting on their own, parsnip, carrot and potato are given a big-time flavor boost when slow-simmered with aromatic spices, fresh ginger and garlic. For added richness, the soup is topped with tangy blue cheese just before serving. Serve this with slices of sourdough bread or Buttermilk Biscuits (page 156).

4½ cups (1.125 L) chicken or vegetable stock

2 Tbsp (30 mL) all-purpose flour

2 garlic cloves, minced

1 medium leek, white and pale green part only, cut in half lengthwise, washed and thinly sliced (see About Leeks on page 197)

1 medium parsnip, peeled, halved lengthwise and sliced

1 medium carrot, peeled, halved lengthwise and sliced

1 medium yam, peeled and cubed

1 Tbsp (15 mL) peeled, chopped fresh ginger (see About Fresh Ginger on page 30)

1 tsp (5 mL) ground cumin

¼ tsp (1 mL) ground coriander

Pinch cayenne pepper

Pinch ground nutmeg

Salt and white pepper to taste

¼ lb (125 g) blue cheese, crumbled

2 Tbsp (30 mL) chopped fresh parsley

Continued . . .

preparation time	•	20 minutes
slow cooker time	•	6 hours
finishing time	•	10 minutes
makes	•	6 servings

ERIC'S OPTIONS
If you find blue cheese too strong, simply omit it or use a milder cheese, such as nuggets of soft goat cheese. For even more richness, sprinkle each serving of soup with 1 Tbsp (15 mL) of toasted chopped walnuts or pecan pieces. To toast the nuts, place ½ cup (125 mL) of your nut of choice in a dry skillet and set over medium heat. Heat the nuts, swirling the pan from time to time, until lightly toasted and aromatic, about 3 to 4 minutes.

Also pictured (left to right): Vegetarian Lentil Soup with Herbes de Provence (page 8) and Split Pea Soup with Smoked Ham and Herbs (page 13).

ROOT VEGETABLE SOUP with BLUE CHEESE
(*continued*)

Place the stock and flour in your slow cooker and whisk until the flour is completely dissolved. Mix in the garlic, leek, parsnip, carrot, yam, ginger, cumin, coriander, cayenne and nutmeg. Cover and cook on the low setting for 6 hours, or until the vegetables are very tender. Purée the contents of the slow cooker with an immersion blender. (You could also purée the soup in a food processor or blender.) Thin the soup with a bit more stock if you find it too thick. Cover and cook for 10 minutes more, or until the soup is piping hot. Season the soup with salt and white pepper. Top bowls of the soup with crumbled blue cheese and chopped parsley.

SPLIT PEA SOUP
with SMOKED HAM and HERBS

Turn this stick-to-your-ribs soup into a filling meal by serving it with buttered slices of Soda Bread with Aged Cheddar, Oats and Green Onions (page 152).

1¾ cups (435 mL) green or yellow split peas

6½ cups (1.625 L) chicken stock

1½ cups (375 mL) diced smoked ham

2 medium celery stalks, finely diced

1 medium onion, finely diced

1 medium carrot, finely diced

2 bay leaves

½ tsp (2.5 mL) ground sage

½ tsp (2.5 mL) dried thyme

½ tsp (2.5 mL) dried marjoram

⅛ tsp (0.5 mL) cayenne pepper

Salt and freshly ground black pepper to taste

2 green onions, thinly sliced

preparation time	•	15 minutes*
slow cooker time	•	6–7 hours
makes	•	8 servings

ERIC'S OPTIONS
Instead of smoked ham, try using diced smoked turkey in this recipe. Or make vegetarian pea soup by omitting the ham and replacing the chicken stock with vegetable stock.

* plus overnight soaking time

Rinse the split peas well in cold water then drain well and place in a large bowl. Cover with 5 cups (1.25 L) of cold water and soak overnight at room temperature.

Drain the peas well and place them in your slow cooker. Mix in the stock, ham, celery, onion, carrot, bay leaves, sage, thyme, marjoram and cayenne. Cover and cook on the low setting for 6 to 7 hours, or until the peas are very tender. Thin the soup with a little more stock if you find it too thick. Season the soup with salt and pepper. Sprinkle servings with sliced green onion.

MULLIGATAWNY SOUP

The curry powder–spiced mix of chicken, vegetables, apple and rice in this classic soup makes it delicious, nutritious and filling. The cooked rice is stirred in at the end of cooking and is only allowed to heat through, otherwise it would overcook, bloat and overly thicken the soup. I like to serve this with wedges of grilled pita or naan bread (see introduction to Spiced Yam and Red Pepper Soup with Yogurt, page 9).

1 lb (500 g) boneless, skinless chicken breast, cut in ¼- to
    ½-inch (6 mm to 1 cm) cubes

4 cups (1 L) chicken stock

2 garlic cloves, minced

1 medium onion, diced

1 medium carrot, diced

1 medium celery stalk, diced

1 small red bell pepper, diced

1 large green apple, diced (skin on)

4 tsp (20 mL) mild or medium curry powder

2 Tbsp (30 mL) fresh lime juice

2 tsp (10 mL) finely grated lime zest

1 Tbsp (15 mL) honey

1 bay leaf

2 Tbsp (30 mL) cornstarch

½ cup (125 mL) cold water

14 oz (398 mL) can regular or light coconut milk

1 cup (250 mL) cooked white or brown rice

¼ cup (60 mL) chopped fresh cilantro or parsley

Salt to taste

preparation time • 25 minutes
slow cooker time • 6 hours
finishing time • 15 minutes
makes • 8 servings

ERIC'S OPTIONS
To make this soup vegetarian, use vegetable stock instead of chicken and replace the chicken with another diced vegetable, such as a small zucchini; or, for added protein, add ½ lb (250 g) of firm tofu, cut into ¼- to ½-inch (6 mm to 1 cm) pieces. If you use tofu, add it when stirring in the rice.

Combine the chicken, stock, garlic, onion, carrot, celery, bell pepper, apple, curry powder, lime juice, lime zest, honey and bay leaf in your slow cooker. Place the cornstarch and cold water in a small bowl. Whisk until it is lump-free then mix into the ingredients in your slow cooker. Cover and cook on the low setting for 6 hours, or until the vegetables are tender. Stir in the coconut milk, rice and cilantro or parsley. Cover and cook for 15 minutes more, or until the soup is piping hot again. Season the soup with salt and serve.

TOMATOEY VEGETABLE SOUP with PASTA and PARMESAN

In this Italian-style recipe, rather than cooking the pasta right in the soup, I spoon hot cooked pasta into bowls before ladling in the soup. This ensures that the pasta will have a nice texture and will not be overcooked and mushy, which can happen if the pasta simmers too long in the soup. Serve this with Roasted Garlic Bread (page 154).

3 cups (750 mL) chicken or vegetable stock

28 oz (796 mL) can diced tomatoes

14 oz (398 mL) can tomato sauce

2 Tbsp (30 mL) tomato paste

2 medium white-skinned potatoes (unpeeled), diced

2 medium garlic cloves, minced

1 medium onion, diced

1 medium carrot, diced

1 large celery stalk, diced

1 green or red bell pepper, diced

1 tsp (5 mL) sugar

2 bay leaves

1 tsp (5 mL) dried oregano

1 tsp (5 mL) dried basil

Salt and freshly ground black pepper to taste

2 cups (500 mL) rotini or other bite-sized pasta

2 Tbsp (30 mL) chopped fresh parsley

Freshly grated Parmesan cheese to taste

Continued . . .

preparation time	•	30 minutes
slow cooker time	•	6 hours*
makes	•	8 servings

ERIC'S OPTIONS
If you would like to add some meat protein to this soup, stir in 1 cup (250 mL) or so of cold, previously cooked diced roast beef, pork, turkey or chicken at the start of cooking.

* includes 10 minutes to cook the pasta

TOMATOEY VEGETABLE SOUP
with PASTA and PARMESAN (*continued*)

Combine the stock, diced tomatoes, tomato sauce, tomato paste, potatoes, garlic, onion, carrot, celery, bell pepper, sugar, bay leaves, oregano and basil in your slow cooker. Cover and cook on the low setting for 6 hours, or until the vegetables are tender. Season the soup with salt and pepper and keep warm in your slow cooker.

When the soup is nearly done, boil the pasta until tender, then drain well. Spoon ⅓ cup (80 mL) or so of the cooked pasta into each bowl of soup you plan to serve. Ladle in the soup and sprinkle with parsley. Let diners sprinkle Parmesan cheese overtop to taste.

Cool any leftover soup to room temperature and stir any leftover pasta into it. Refrigerate and enjoy the soup over the next day or two, or freeze. When freezing, package the soup in portion sizes that best suit your needs. For example, if your plan is to take the soup for a workday lunch, freeze it in small, single-serving portions. If you want to have 2 portions of soup for a Saturday lunch with your spouse, freeze it in containers that hold that amount. Thaw the soup overnight in the refrigerator before reheating.

BEEFY BORSCHT with HORSERADISH SOUR CREAM

Sour cream tastes great spooned on borscht. Horse-radish is, of course, a classic condiment for beef. Combine the two and you have the perfect topping for this chunky, stew-like soup. I like to serve this with slices of dark rye bread.

2 lb (1 kg) beets (without tops)

6 cups (1.5 L) beef stock

2 cups (500 mL) cooked, cubed roast beef

2 medium white-skinned potatoes (unpeeled), diced

2 medium garlic cloves, minced

1 medium onion, diced

1 medium carrot, diced

1 large celery stalk, diced

2 bay leaves

½ cup (125 mL) regular or low-fat sour cream

2 Tbsp (30 mL) prepared horseradish, or to taste

⅓ lb (170 g) green beans, blanched and sliced (see Note)

1 Tbsp (15 mL) chopped fresh dill

Salt and freshly ground black pepper to taste

Continued . . .

preparation time •	30 minutes*
slow cooker time •	7–8 hours
finishing time •	10 minutes
makes •	8–10 servings

NOTE
To blanch beans, plunge them into boiling water for 1 minute. Drain well, cool in ice-cold water and drain well again.

ERIC'S OPTIONS
1 tsp (5 mL) of dried dill could replace the fresh dill in this recipe. Because it's dried, add it to the soup at the start of cooking so that it can slowly reconstitute itself as the soup cooks.

* plus boiling time for beets

BEEFY BORSCHT with
HORSERADISH SOUR CREAM (*continued*)

Place the beets in a pot, cover with cold water and boil until tender, 30 to 40 minutes, depending on their size. Drain well then cool them in ice-cold water. Peel off the skins when cool. They should just slip off. Cut the beets into ¼- to ½-inch (6 mm to 1 cm) cubes and place in your slow cooker. Mix in the stock, beef, potatoes, garlic, onion, carrot, celery and bay leaves. Cover and cook on the low setting for 7 to 8 hours, or until the vegetables are tender. While the soup cooks, combine the sour cream and horseradish in a bowl. Cover and refrigerate until needed.

After 7 to 8 hours of cooking, if the vegetables are tender (longer if not), stir in the green beans, dill and salt and pepper. Cover and cook for 10 minutes more, or until the beans are heated through, then serve. Set the horseradish-flavored sour cream on the table and allow diners to dollop it on their borscht to taste.

DARK and RICH ONION SOUP with SWISS CHEESE CROUTONS

Slow-cooking the onions on the stovetop for 15 minutes makes them golden, sweet and delicious. They then turn dark and delicious when cooked in the slow cooker with additions such as red wine and beef stock. The thick, cheese-topped crouton makes this soup filling enough to serve as a main course, but you could certainly serve a salad alongside or to start. Butter Lettuce Salad with Walnuts and Dried Cherries (page 164) would be perfect.

2 Tbsp (30 mL) butter

2 Tbsp (30 mL) olive oil

4 medium yellow onions, halved and thinly sliced

4 cups (1 L) beef stock

1 cup (250 mL) red wine

3 Tbsp (45 mL) Dijon mustard

2 tsp (10 mL) minced fresh thyme

1 bay leaf

1 tsp (5 mL) Worcestershire sauce

Salt and freshly ground black pepper to taste

6 thick slices of French bread (see Note)

⅓ lb (170 g) Swiss cheese, grated (see Note)

Chopped fresh parsley to taste

preparation time	•	25 minutes
slow cooker time	•	6 hours*
finishing time	•	5 minutes
makes	•	6 servings

NOTE

The loaf of French bread I used for this recipe was about 6 inches (15 cm) wide. If you've bought a bag of pre-grated cheese, 1¼ cups (310 mL) should match the ⅓ lb (170 g) required for this recipe.

ERIC'S OPTIONS

If you don't want to use wine, you can simply replace it with more beef stock. Or, instead of beef stock, you could use chicken stock, or even vegetable stock if you're vegetarian. Note that chicken and vegetable stock won't give the soup as rich or dark a color, though.

* includes 15 minutes to prepare croutons

Place the butter and oil in a wide skillet or pot set over medium heat. When the butter has melted, add the onions and cook, stirring occasionally, until they are very tender, golden and sticky, about 15 minutes. Spoon the onions into your slow cooker. Mix in the stock, wine, mustard, thyme, bay leaf and Worcestershire sauce. Cover and cook on the low setting for 6 hours. Season the soup with salt and pepper. Cover and keep the soup warm in the slow cooker.

When the soup is nearly done, preheat the oven to 400°F (200°C). Line a baking sheet with parchment paper.

Set the bread slices on the prepared baking sheet. Bake the bread for 8 minutes, then turn each slice over. Top each slice with an equal amount of the cheese. Bake for 5 minutes more, or until the cheese is melted and the bread crispy on the bottom. Ladle the soup into wide, shallow bowls. Set a Swiss cheese crouton in the center of each bowl and serve, sprinkled with chopped parsley.

WHY DO ONIONS MAKE YOU CRY?

Many folks cry when they chop onions—but not because they are sad. Inside an onion are cells that contain highly volatile sulfur compounds. When you chop an onion, those compounds are released into the air and, if they reach your eyes, can cause tearing. The best way to minimize your tears is to keep your onions refrigerated in a tightly sealed plastic bag. When an onion is cold, its sulfur compounds are less volatile. If you store your onions at room temperature, chill them in the freezer for 10 minutes before chopping, if time allows. Also, be sure to use a sharp knife. A dull one will crush the onion and release more of those compounds into the air.

BARLEY SOUP with LAMB, LEEKS and POTATOES

I usually make this hearty soup the day after I've cooked a roast leg of lamb. It's a great way to turn the leftover meat into another satisfying meal. Make a fine feast of this soup by serving it with buttered slices of Soda Bread with Aged Cheddar, Oats and Green Onions (page 152).

preparation time	•	20 minutes
slow cooker time	•	6–7 hours
makes	•	8 servings

ERIC'S OPTIONS
Instead of lamb, use cubes of leftover cooked beef.

6 cups (1.5 L) beef stock

2 cups (500 mL) cubed cooked lamb

¾ cup (185 mL) pot barley

3 medium white-skinned potatoes (unpeeled), cubed

2 medium celery stalks, finely diced

2 garlic cloves, minced

1 large leek, white and pale green part only, cut in half lengthwise, washed and thinly sliced (see About Leeks on page 197)

1 medium carrot, finely diced

3 Tbsp (45 mL) tomato paste

1 Tbsp (15 mL) Worcestershire sauce

2 bay leaves

½ tsp (2.5 mL) dried thyme

Salt and freshly ground black pepper to taste

Chopped fresh parsley to taste

Combine the stock, lamb, barley, potatoes, celery, garlic, leek, carrot, tomato paste, Worcestershire sauce, bay leaves and thyme in your slow cooker. Cover and cook on the low setting for 6 to 7 hours, or until the lamb and barley are tender. Season the soup with salt and pepper. Sprinkle servings of the soup with chopped fresh parsley.

ABOUT PEARL AND POT BARLEY

The two main types of barley you'll see for sale in supermarkets are pearl barley and pot barley.

With pearl barley, the grain is polished to remove the tough bran portion and the germ. This process gives the grain a pearl-like finish, hence its name. Without the bran it cooks fairly quickly and is tender to the bite, but it is also lower in nutritional value. However, it still contains important vitamins and minerals and is a good source of fiber, with ½ cup (125 mL) of pearl barley providing more than 50 percent of an adult's daily requirement.

The grain of pot barley is also polished to remove the tough bran, but the polishing is not as intense and more of the whole grain is left intact. This makes it a little more nutrient-rich than pearl barley and a little chewier once cooked. For slow cooker recipes, I prefer pot barley to pearl barley. It holds its shape better and has a nicer texture.

VEGETARIAN

YAM STEW with PEAS and GINGER

Yams are the main ingredient in this ginger-rich stew and that can only be a good thing. These tasty, nutritious tubers contain fiber, protein, iron, calcium and vitamins A and C. Serve the stew on a bed of rice, either simply steamed or dressed up. Jasmine Fried Rice (page 180) is delicious with this.

14 oz (398 mL) can regular or light coconut milk

1 Tbsp (15 mL) cornstarch

28 oz (796 mL) can diced tomatoes

1 cup (250 mL) chicken or vegetable stock

3 medium yams, peeled, quartered lengthwise and sliced into 1-inch (2.5 cm) pieces

2 garlic cloves, minced

1 medium onion, halved and sliced

2 Tbsp (30 mL) peeled, chopped fresh ginger (see About Fresh Ginger on page 30)

1½ Tbsp (22.5 mL) mild or medium curry powder

20 snow or snap peas, blanched and halved widthwise (see Note)

Salt to taste

Chopped fresh cilantro or sliced green onion to taste

preparation time	• 25 minutes
slow cooker time	• 5–6 hours
finishing time	• 10 minutes
makes	• 6–8 servings

NOTE

To blanch the snow or snap peas, plunge them into boiling water for 1 minute. Drain well, cool in ice-cold water, then drain well again.

ERIC'S OPTIONS

Instead of yams, try 4 cups (1 L) of cubed squash in this recipe. Banana or butternut squash works well.

Place the coconut milk and cornstarch in your slow cooker and whisk to combine. Mix in the diced tomatoes, stock, yams, garlic, onion, ginger and curry powder. Cover and cook on the low setting for 5 to 6 hours, or until the yams are tender. Stir in the peas, cover and cook for 10 minutes more, or until the peas are heated through. Season the stew with salt. Sprinkle servings of the stew with cilantro or sliced green onion.

ABOUT SWEET POTATOES AND YAMS

Most supermarkets have sections for sweet potatoes and yams, but the truth is, they are selling only sweet potatoes. What is labeled a "yam" in most stores is in fact an orange-fleshed variety of sweet potato. True yams are a staple ingredient in many Asian countries and are not widely available for sale in North America. This tropical tuber is sweeter and much larger than a sweet potato, growing up to 3 feet (90 cm) or more in length.

Years ago, a savvy food marketer decided to call the orange-fleshed variety of sweet potato a yam. The goal, which was achieved, was to help distinguish it from the other, more commonly grown variety, which has tan-colored skin and pale yellow flesh and is correctly labeled as a sweet potato in stores.

Beyond being similar in shape, these two types of sweet potato are quite different in taste, texture and preparation requirements. The yellow-fleshed variety is floury like a baking potato and lighter when cooked, which makes it well suited for baking, mashing and cutting into sticks and deep-frying. Orange-fleshed sweet potatoes are much denser in texture, not unlike a waxy red- or white-skinned potato. That quality makes it well suited for dishes where you want it to hold its shape, such as ones that call for slices or cubes of it to be cooked in a casserole or stew.

ABOUT FRESH GINGER

Ginger is the tan-colored, knobby rhizome of a perennial herb whose botanical name is *Zingiber officinale*. The plant can grow more than 3 feet (90 cm) tall and when the leaves die, the rhizome is harvested and sold as ginger. On a flavor-to-cost ratio, fresh ginger is one heck of a deal. It's inexpensive and just a small amount can add a world of flavor to all sorts of dishes.

When purchasing ginger, look for firm pieces with fairly smooth skin. If it appears shriveled or has spongy spots, it's old or was improperly stored and should be avoided. It will be difficult to peel, cut or grate.

Unpeeled fresh ginger, if placed in a tightly sealed plastic bag, can be kept in your refrigerator crisper for up to 3 weeks, depending on how fresh it was when purchased. For the freshest ginger taste, buy only what you can use within a reasonable length of time.

If for some reason you've purchased a pile of fresh ginger, you could place it in a tightly sealed plastic bag and freeze it for up to 2 months. Slice, chop or grate the ginger when still partially frozen, as it will be harder to do so when thawed. Another option for longer-term storage is to peel and slice the ginger, place it in a jar, top it with sake, dry sherry or vodka, tightly screw on the lid and store it in the refrigerator for a month or more. Note that both these processes will alter the original lively, fresh ginger taste.

FALL VEGETABLE and BEAN STEW

Enjoy this stew's flavorful sauce to the max by serving it on a bed of rice, such as Rice Pilaf with Thyme, Lemon and Garlic (page 183), which will soak up all the juices.

2 cups (500 mL) vegetable stock

2 Tbsp (30 mL) all-purpose flour

19 oz (540 mL) can white kidney beans, drained, rinsed in cold water and drained again

14 oz (398 mL) can diced tomatoes

2 cups (500 mL) cubed squash (banana or butternut works well)

2 garlic cloves, minced

1 medium onion, halved and sliced

1 medium parsnip, quartered lengthwise and sliced

1 medium zucchini, quartered lengthwise and sliced

2 Tbsp (30 mL) tomato paste

1 tsp (5 mL) dried thyme leaves

1 tsp (5 mL) ground cumin

¼ tsp (1 mL) sweet paprika (see About Paprika on page 71)

Pinch crushed chili flakes

Salt and freshly ground black pepper to taste

2 Tbsp (30 mL) chopped fresh parsley

preparation time •	20 minutes
slow cooker time •	5–6 hours
makes •	6 servings

ERIC'S OPTIONS
Instead of squash, try cubes of yams or sweet potatoes in this recipe. Instead of white kidney beans, try another canned legume, such as chickpeas.

Place the stock and flour in your slow cooker and whisk until the flour is completely dissolved. Mix in the beans, diced tomatoes, squash, garlic, onion, parsnip, zucchini, tomato paste, thyme, cumin, paprika and chili flakes. Cover and cook on the low setting for 5 to 6 hours, or until the vegetables are tender. Season the stew with salt and pepper. Sprinkle servings of the stew with parsley.

SQUASH and BLACK BEAN CHILI

This chili is bursting with cubes of orangey squash and with other vegetables, beans and spices. Who needs meat? This dish tastes so good you'll want another bowl, even if you're a confirmed meat-eater. Serve this with Cornbread with Pepper Jack Cheese (pictured; recipe page 159).

preparation time • 25 minutes
slow cooker time • 6 hours
makes • 6–8 serving

ERIC'S OPTIONS
Like I suggest for the Tex-Mex Turkey Chili (page 89), dress up bowls of this squash chili with sour cream and grated Monterey Jack or cheddar cheese. Instead of squash, use 4 cups (1 L) of cubed yam or sweet potato in this recipe. For a spicier chili, add a large jalapeño pepper, seeds removed and flesh finely chopped, at the beginning of cooking.

28 oz (796 mL) can diced tomatoes

14 oz (398 mL) can tomato sauce

1 cup (250 mL) vegetable stock or beer

4 cups (1 L) peeled, cubed banana or butternut squash

19 oz (540 mL) can black beans, drained, rinsed in cold water and drained again

1 medium onion, diced

1 medium green bell pepper, diced

1 cup (250 mL) fresh or frozen corn kernels

1–2 garlic cloves, minced

2 tsp (10 mL) chili powder

1 tsp (5 mL) ground cumin

1 tsp (5 mL) dried oregano

Hot pepper sauce to taste

Salt and freshly ground black pepper to taste

3 Tbsp (45 mL) chopped fresh cilantro or sliced green onion

Combine the diced tomatoes, tomato sauce, stock or beer, squash, black beans, onion, bell pepper, corn, garlic, chili powder, cumin, oregano and hot pepper sauce in your slow cooker. Cover and cook on the low setting for 6 hours, or until the vegetables are tender. Season the chili with salt and pepper. Sprinkle servings of the stew with cilantro or sliced green onion.

CHICKPEA VEGETABLE STEW
with APRICOTS and RAISINS

This vegetarian stew is flavored North African–style with ingredients such as cumin, lemon and apricots. I like to serve it over hot couscous (see Eric's Options).

19 oz (540 mL) can chickpeas, drained, rinsed in cold water and drained again

14 oz (398 mL) can diced tomatoes

14 oz (398 mL) can tomato sauce

1 cup (250 mL) vegetable stock

2 Tbsp (30 mL) olive oil

1 medium onion, diced

1 medium carrot, quartered lengthwise and sliced

1 small zucchini, quartered lengthwise and sliced

2 garlic cloves, minced

8–10 dried apricots, thinly sliced

¼ cup (60 mL) raisins

2 tsp (10 mL) grated lemon zest

1 tsp (5 mL) ground cumin

¼ tsp (1 mL) cayenne pepper

2 Tbsp (30 mL) chopped fresh mint, cilantro or parsley

Salt and freshly ground black pepper to taste

preparation time	• 20 minutes
slow cooker time	• 6 hours
makes	• 4 servings

ERIC'S OPTIONS
If you're not vegetarian, you could use chicken stock instead of vegetable stock in this recipe, if that's what you have on hand or prefer. To serve the stew on a bed of couscous, place 3 cups (750 mL) of vegetable stock, 1 Tbsp (15 mL) olive oil and 1 minced garlic clove in a medium-sized pot and bring to a boil. Mix in 1¾ cups (435 mL) of couscous. Cover the pot with its lid, turn off the heat and let the couscous stand for 5 minutes. Fluff the couscous with a fork to separate the grains and then serve.

Combine the chickpeas, diced tomatoes, tomato sauce, stock, olive oil, onion, carrot, zucchini, garlic, apricots, raisins, lemon zest, cumin and cayenne in your slow cooker. Cover and cook on the low setting for 6 hours, or until the vegetables are tender. Stir in the mint. Season with salt and pepper and serve.

HOT SWEET-and-SOUR VEGETABLES with EDAMAME

Edamame is the Japanese name for fresh soybeans. You can buy them fresh or frozen in their pods, or shelled and frozen. I used shelled and frozen in this recipe, a convenient, healthy, ready-to-use ingredient sold at most supermarkets. Try stirring it into Asian-style dishes such as this one to add a rich green hue. This dish has many flavors and ingredients, so I like to serve it with a simple side dish such as steamed long-grain white or brown rice.

14 oz (398 mL) can crushed tomatoes

1½ cups (375 mL) vegetable stock

¼ cup (60 mL) packed golden brown sugar

2 Tbsp (30 mL) rice vinegar

2 Tbsp (30 mL) soy sauce

2 tsp (10 mL) hot Asian-style chili sauce, or to taste

1 tsp (5 mL) cornstarch

14 oz (398 mL) can cut miniature (baby) corn, drained well

7½ oz (213 mL) can sliced water chestnuts, drained well

1 medium carrot, halved lengthwise and sliced on the bias

1 medium green bell pepper, cut into ½-inch (1 cm) cubes

1 medium onion, cut into ½-inch (1 cm) cubes

1–2 garlic cloves, minced

1 Tbsp (15 mL) peeled, chopped fresh ginger (see About Fresh Ginger on page 30)

1½ cups (375 mL) frozen shelled edamame, thawed

3 baby bok choy, coarsely chopped (See About Bok Choy on facing page)

2–3 green onions, thinly sliced

preparation time	•	20 minutes
slow cooker time	•	4–5 hours
finishing time	•	10–15 minut
makes	•	6–8 serving:

ERIC'S OPTIONS

If you can't find edamame, you could use 20 snow or snap peas, each cut in half widthwise and blanched. Mix in the peas when you add the edamame and cover and heat them through for 10 minutes. To blanch the peas, plunge them into boiling water for 1 minute. Drain well, cool in ice-cold water and drain well again.

Place the crushed tomatoes, stock, brown sugar, vinegar, soy sauce, chili sauce and cornstarch in your slow cooker and whisk to combine. Mix in the corn, water chestnuts, carrot, bell pepper, onion, garlic and ginger. Cover and cook on the low setting for 4 to 5 hours, or until the vegetables are tender. Stir in the edamame and bok choy and cook for 10 to 15 minutes more, or until the edamame is heated through and the bok choy wilted. Sprinkle servings of the vegetables with sliced green onion.

ABOUT BOK CHOY

Bok choy is a mild-tasting member of the brassica family, which includes cabbage and broccoli. It has smooth, white or pale green stalks topped with dark green leaves. Bok choy is sold as a full-sized, mature plant, about the size of a medium head of romaine. It's also sold as baby bok choy, which is a smaller, not fully mature version of the same vegetable about 4 to 6 inches (10 to 15 cm) long.

When buying either type of bok choy, look for crack-free, firm stalks topped with lively, bright leaves. Store in a plastic bag in the vegetable crisper. Bok choy, like lettuce, is fairly perishable and should be used within a few days of purchase. Wash bok choy well before using; there are crevices in its stalks and leaves where dirt can get trapped.

VEGETABLE TIKKA MASALA

This is a vegetarian version of a dish made famous in Britain. It's usually made with chicken. The whipping cream in the curry-laced sauce in which the vegetables are cooked gives it a silky texture and, of course, a divinely rich taste. I like to serve this dish with slices of cumin seed flatbread (see Eric's Options for Rosemary Flatbread on page 161).

1 cup (250 mL) tomato sauce

1 cup (250 mL) vegetable stock or water

1 cup (250 mL) whipping (35%) cream

2–3 Tbsp (30–45 mL) mild, medium or hot curry powder

1 tsp (5 mL) cornstarch

18 small to medium cauliflower florets

10–12 miniature red-skinned potatoes, each quartered

1 medium carrot, halved lengthwise and sliced on the bias

1 green bell pepper, diced

1 medium onion, diced

2 Tbsp (30 mL) peeled, chopped fresh ginger (see About Fresh Ginger on page 30)

2–3 garlic cloves, minced

1 cup (250 mL) frozen peas

Salt to taste

3 Tbsp (45 mL) chopped fresh cilantro or sliced green onion

preparation time	•	20 minutes
slow cooker time	•	5–6 hours
finishing time	•	10 minutes
makes	•	6 servings

ERIC'S OPTIONS
If you can't have dairy, replace the whipping cream with an equal amount of coconut milk.

Place the tomato sauce, stock, cream, curry powder and cornstarch in your slow cooker and whisk to combine. Mix in the cauliflower, potatoes, carrot, bell pepper, onion, ginger and garlic. The mixture will look thick, but moisture will seep out of the vegetables as they cook, so don't be tempted to add extra liquid. Push down on the potatoes to ensure they are submerged in the liquid. Cover and cook on the low setting for 5 to 6 hours, or until the vegetables are tender. Mix in the peas, cover and cook for 10 minutes more, or just until the peas are heated through. Season the tikka masala with salt. Sprinkle servings with chopped cilantro or sliced green onion.

ABOUT TIKKA MASALA

Britain's love affair with Indian food has reached such a peak that one very popular creation invented in that country is now considered a national dish: chicken tikka masala. The story goes that, a few decades ago, a customer in a Glaswegian curry house asked for gravy with his Indian-style chicken. The chef obliged by topping the chicken with a quickly prepared spicy tomato sauce and chicken tikka masala was born.

In culinary terms, "tikka" means pieces or cubes of meat. Masala is a spice mixture used to flavor sauces. For chicken tikka masala, the meat is simply simmered in a sauce flavored with masala. I have read dozens of masala sauce recipes and realized that you could substitute pieces or cubes of vegetables for the chicken for a vegetarian alternative.

BARLEY RISOTTO with GRILLED ASPARAGUS

Unlike many slow cooker recipes that can sit a while and stay warm in your slow cooker until you are ready to eat, this one cannot. The barley will overcook and turn mushy if you let this dish sit. Not a good thing. The benefit of cooking the risotto in the slow cooker is that you can relax or get some chores done, such as setting the table, during the first 90 minutes of cooking time while it cooks unattended. You could serve a salad before or alongside the risotto, such as Romaine Hearts with Focaccia Croutons and Parmesan (page 169).

2 Tbsp (30 mL) olive oil

1 medium leek, white and pale green part only, halved lengthwise, washed and thinly sliced (see About Leeks on page 197)

3½ cups (875 mL) vegetable stock

1 cup (250 mL) pot barley

½ cup (125 mL) dry white wine

8 oil-packed sun-dried tomatoes, drained well and thinly sliced

2 garlic cloves, minced

20 asparagus spears, stems trimmed

Olive oil for brushing

⅓ cup (80 mL) freshly grated Parmesan cheese

¼ cup (60 mL) chopped fresh basil

Salt and freshly ground black pepper to taste

preparation time	•	15 minutes
slow cooker time	•	2½ hours
makes	•	4 servings

ERIC'S OPTIONS
Place a wedge of Parmesan cheese on a plate and set on your dining room table with a grater. Also set a good bottle of olive oil there. Your diners can use these to richen the flavor of the risotto if they desire.

Place the 2 Tbsp (30 mL) oil in a skillet set over medium heat. When hot, add the leek and cook until tender, about 5 minutes. Spoon the leek into your slow cooker. Mix in the stock, barley, wine, sun-dried tomatoes and garlic. Cover and cook on the low setting for 90 minutes. Stir the barley and cook for 1 hour more, or until the barley is just tender.

When the barley is 20 minutes from being ready, preheat your grill to medium-high. Preheat the oven to 200°F (95°C).

Lightly brush the asparagus with olive oil. Grill the asparagus for 1 minute per side, or until lightly charred. Set in a baking dish and keep warm in the oven until the risotto is ready.

When the barley has cooked for the 2 hours and 30 minutes and/or is tender, stir in the Parmesan cheese, basil and salt and pepper. To serve, divide the risotto among 4 serving bowls and top with asparagus.

ROMANO BEANS with TOMATOES, ARUGULA and GOAT CHEESE

This Mediterranean-style bean dish is both colorful and flavorful with its spicy, emerald green arugula, sweet, rich red cherry tomatoes and tangy, creamy-colored goat cheese. I like to serve it with slices of focaccia or olive bread.

Two 19 oz (540 mL) cans romano beans, drained, rinsed in cold water and drained again

1 cup (250 mL) vegetable stock

½ cup (125 mL) dry white wine

18 cherry tomatoes, halved

1 medium green bell pepper, diced

½ medium onion, diced

Crushed chili flakes to taste

2 Tbsp (30 mL) olive oil

3 Tbsp (45 mL) pesto

3–4 cups (750 mL–1 L) baby arugula (see About Arugula on page 44)

Salt and freshly ground black pepper to taste

6 oz (175 g) soft goat cheese, crumbled

preparation time	•	20 minutes
slow cooker time	•	5–6 hours
finishing time	•	3–4 minutes
makes	•	6 servings

ERIC'S OPTIONS
If you can't find romano beans, use white kidney beans in this recipe instead. Instead of goat cheese, try crumbled feta cheese.

Place the beans, stock, wine, tomatoes, bell pepper, onion, chili flakes and olive oil in your slow cooker and mix to combine. Cover and cook on the low setting for 5 to 6 hours, or until the tomatoes are quite soft. Mix in the pesto, arugula and salt and pepper. Cover and cook for 3 to 4 minutes more, or just until the arugula is wilted. Top the servings of beans with crumbled goat cheese.

ABOUT ARUGULA

Arugula, also known as rocket, is a member of the cabbage family. It is related to a variety of other strong-tasting plants, such as watercress. I think of it as a leafy green with attitude. Unlike some tender greens, its peppery flavor is bold enough to be used in both hot and cold preparations and its spicy, intriguing taste will certainly make you notice it's there.

Arugula is sold in bunches with the roots attached, or as loose leaves with the roots trimmed off. Baby arugula is simply arugula picked when young. Its leaves are smaller and taste less intense.

Buy arugula that has bright, fresh-looking, green leaves. To store arugula with the roots still attached, wrap the roots in slightly dampened paper towel, place the arugula in a plastic bag and refrigerate. If very fresh, it should keep for a few days. Loose leaves of arugula can be stored in a tightly sealed plastic bag, or in the plastic box it was sold in, in the refrigerator.

When ready to use, trim off the roots, if still attached, thoroughly wash the arugula in cold water and dry on clean towels.

As you enjoy your arugula, you can also enjoy knowing that it is a source of iron, calcium and vitamins A and C.

RATATOUILLE with FRESH BASIL and OLIVE OIL

This is a slow-cooked version of the classic vegetable dish from the south of France. Ironically, I like to serve this saucy creation Italian-style, spooned over pasta, such as rigatoni, with Roasted Garlic Bread (page 154) alongside.

preparation time	•	20 minutes
slow cooker time	•	5–6 hours
makes	•	6–8 servings

ERIC'S OPTIONS

If you don't want to use wine, add the equivalent volume of vegetable stock. For a spicy taste, stir crushed chili flakes to taste into the ratatouille at the start of cooking.

14 oz (398 mL) can crushed tomatoes

14 oz (398 mL) can diced tomatoes

½ cup (125 mL) dry white wine

½ cup (125 mL) vegetable stock

1 Tbsp (15 mL) golden brown sugar

1 medium onion, diced

1 medium yellow bell pepper, diced

1 medium green bell pepper, diced

1 small eggplant, cut into ½-inch (1 cm) cubes

1 small zucchini, cut into ½-inch (1 cm) cubes

½ lb (250 g) brown or white mushrooms, each halved (see Buying and Storing White and Brown Mushrooms on page 121)

2 garlic cloves, minced

2 Tbsp (30 mL) extra virgin olive oil

12–16 fresh basil leaves, cut into thin slices

⅓ cup (80 mL) freshly grated Parmesan cheese

Salt and freshly ground black pepper to taste

Place the crushed tomatoes, diced tomatoes, wine, stock and sugar in your slow cooker and mix to combine. Mix in the onion, bell peppers, eggplant, zucchini, mushrooms and garlic. The ratatouille will look like it needs additional liquid, but as the vegetables cook moisture will seep out of them, creating a saucy mixture around the vegetables. Cover and cook on the low setting for 5 to 6 hours, or until the vegetables are tender. Mix in the oil, basil, cheese and salt and pepper and serve.

SAVOY CABBAGE ROLLS
with TOASTED ALMONDS

The bright green leaves of savoy cabbage used in this recipe are filled with a tasty rice mixture strewn with mushrooms and mixed vegetables. The almonds are sprinkled on the cabbage rolls after plating, adding a nice crunchy texture to this dish. I like to serve these with store-bought or homemade pickled beets, such as Pickled Beets with Balsamic and Spice (page 174).

2 Tbsp (30 mL) olive oil

⅓ lb (175 g) brown mushrooms, thinly sliced (see Buying and Storing White and Brown Mushrooms on page 121)

1 medium onion, finely diced

½ medium green bell pepper, finely diced

½ cup (125 mL) grated carrot

1 large garlic clove, minced

10 savoy cabbage leaves, each about 5 inches (12 cm) wide

2 cups (500 mL) cooked white or brown rice, cold

1 large egg, beaten

1 tsp (5 mL) dried sage leaves (see Note)

Salt and freshly ground black pepper to taste

1¾ cups (435 mL) vegetable stock

14 oz (398 mL) can crushed tomatoes

½ cup (125 mL) unsweetened apple juice

⅓ cup (80 mL) sliced almonds, lightly toasted (see Note)

preparation time	•	30 minutes
slow cooker time	•	6 hours
finishing time	•	5 minutes
makes	•	4 servings*

NOTE

In this book, the dried herb I call sage leaves is dried whole sage leaves, which are crumbled into small but discernible pieces and bottled or sold in bags most often labeled "sage leaves." Do not substitute ground sage, which is a finely ground powder and much more intense in flavor.

To toast the almonds, place them in a single layer in a small baking pan and bake in a preheated 325°F (160°C) oven, stirring occasionally, for 10 to 15 minutes, or until lightly toasted.

* 2 cabbage rolls each

Heat the oil in a skillet set over medium heat. Add the mushrooms, onion, pepper, carrot and garlic and cook until tender and any liquid from the mushrooms has evaporated. Spoon the mixture into a bowl and cool to room temperature.

Meanwhile, bring a large pot of water to a boil. Add the cabbage leaves and cook until just tender, 2 to 3 minutes. Cool in ice-cold water, drain well and pat dry. Trim off the lower part of the tough vein running through the center of each leaf and discard.

Mix the rice, egg, sage and salt and pepper into the mushroom/vegetable mixture.

Line the bottom of your slow cooker with 2 of the cabbage leaves. Set the remaining cabbage leaves, curved side down, on a work surface.

Spoon an equal amount of the rice into the center of each cabbage leaf on the work surface. Fold the sides of the cabbage leaves over the filling and tightly roll. Set the cabbage rolls, seam side down, in your slow cooker.

Combine the stock, crushed tomatoes and apple juice in a bowl. Pour over the cabbage rolls. Cook on the low setting for 6 hours, or until the cabbage rolls are tender. Set 2 cabbage rolls on each plate. Spoon over the sauce in the slow cooker, sprinkle with almonds and enjoy.

FISH AND SEAFOOD

POACHED FISH in a SAFFRON, ORANGE and FENNEL BROTH

The broth of stock, wine, citrus and slices of anise-flavored fennel develops a splendid flavor as it slowly simmers. The fish added near the end of cooking takes 6 to 8 minutes to poach. While it does, the saffron in the broth turns the fish a beautiful golden yellow color. Serve the fish with your favorite green vegetable and boiled potatoes.

preparation time •	10 minutes
slow cooker time •	4 hours
finishing time •	6–8 minutes
makes •	4 servings

ERIC'S OPTIONS
Any remaining poaching liquid could be strained, cooled to room temperature, packaged and frozen. Thaw and use in recipes calling for fish stock, or bring to a simmer and use to steam open mussels or clams.

3 cups (750 mL) fish or chicken stock

½ cup (125 mL) dry white wine

½ cup (125 mL) orange juice

2 garlic cloves, halved and thinly sliced

1 small fresh fennel bulb, quartered lengthwise and thinly sliced (see Buying and Storing Fresh Fennel on facing page)

½ tsp (2.5 mL) loosely packed saffron threads, crumbled

8 whole black peppercorns

Four 6 oz (175 g) halibut, salmon or cod fillets

Salt and white pepper to taste

Fresh fennel leaves for garnish (optional)

Combine the stock, wine, juice, garlic, sliced fennel bulb, saffron and peppercorns in your slow cooker. Cover and cook on the low setting for 4 hours. Quickly submerge the fish in the poaching liquid. Cover and cook for 6 to 8 minutes more, or until the fish is just cooked through. Carefully lift the fish out of the poaching liquid and onto dinner plates or shallow-sided bowls. Season the poaching liquid with salt and white pepper. Spoon some of the poaching liquid, including pieces of the fennel, over the fish. Garnish with fresh fennel leaves, if desired, and serve.

BUYING AND STORING FRESH FENNEL

When buying fresh fennel, look for plants with firm, crack-free, almost bright-looking bulbs with ultrafresh-looking frilly leaves. In my experience, large, wide fennel bulbs are more tender than long, slender ones. You can store fennel in a plastic bag in your refrigerator crisper for 3 to 5 days, but its flavor will lose some of its anise-like punch if it sits too long.

Wash fennel thoroughly before using; it has lots of crevices where dirt can get trapped. To prepare fennel for cooking, or for using it raw, trim off the tough upper stems and remove the core at the bottom of the plant. The stalks making up the outer surface of the bulb can sometimes form a tough skin. In that case, use a vegetable peeler to remove a thin layer of the tough outer skin, leaving the rest of the stalk intact and good to use.

POACHED SALMON with MUSTARD TARRAGON SAUCE

A slow cooker is perfect for poaching fish fillets. In this slow-simmering environment, the fish cooks very gently, ensuring it holds its shape and absorbs all the tasty flavors in the poaching liquid. Serve this salmon and rich sauce on a bed of Garlic Mashed Yukon Gold Potatoes with Kale (pictured; recipe page 194).

preparation time	•	20 minutes
slow cooker time	•	4 hours*
finishing time	•	6–8 minutes
makes	•	4 servings

3 cups (750 mL) chicken or fish stock

2 cups (500 mL) water

1 medium onion, halved and thinly sliced

2 Tbsp (30 mL) fresh lemon juice

8 whole black peppercorns

2 garlic cloves, halved and thinly sliced

2 bay leaves

4 fresh parsley sprigs

2–3 fresh thyme sprigs

1 cup (250 mL) dry white wine, divided

½ tsp (2.5 mL) dried tarragon

1½ cups (375 mL) whipping (35%) cream

¼ cup (60 mL) whole grain Dijon mustard

Salt and white pepper to taste

Four 6 oz (175 g) salmon fillets

Continued . . .

ERIC'S OPTIONS

Instead of salmon fillets, try halibut or other firm fish fillets with this sauce. Instead of dried tarragon, use 2 tsp (10 mL) of freshly chopped tarragon in the sauce, stirring it in after the sauce has thickened to preserve its rich green color. Any remaining poaching liquid could be strained, cooled to room temperature, packaged and frozen. Thaw and use in recipes calling for fish stock, or bring to a simmer and use to steam open mussels or clams.

* includes 10 minutes to make the sauce

POACHED SALMON with MUSTARD TARRAGON SAUCE
(*continued*)

Combine the stock, water, onion, lemon juice, peppercorns, garlic, bay leaves, parsley, thyme and ½ cup (125 mL) of the wine in your slow cooker. Cover and cook on the low setting for 4 hours.

When the poaching liquid has cooked for 3 hours 50 minutes, place the remaining ½ cup (125 mL) of wine and the tarragon in a small pot and set over medium-high heat. Simmer to reduce the wine by half. Pour in the cream and simmer to reduce until a slightly thickened sauce forms. It should be able to coat the back of a spoon. Stir in the mustard and salt and pepper and reserve on low heat.

When the poaching liquid has cooked for 4 hours, quickly submerge the salmon in it. Cover and cook for 6 to 8 minutes more, or until the fish is just cooked through. Carefully lift the salmon out of the poaching liquid and onto serving plates. Top with the sauce and serve.

WHEN IS FISH COOKED?

Fish is cooked when the translucent flesh becomes opaque and its flakes begin to separate very slightly and pull apart. With fattier fish, such as salmon, white deposits of fat will often seep out between the flakes when the fish is cooked. Cooked fish should feel slightly firm. If it feels hard, that's a sign you've overcooked it; if it's soft and spongy, it's not cooked through.

SALMON STEW with DILL

I adapted this recipe from a chicken stew recipe. The main difference is that, whereas the chicken simmers for a while in the stew, the quick-cooking salmon is added near the end of cooking. I like to serve this stew on a bed of Leek and Red Potato Mashers (page 196).

preparation time	•	15 minutes
slow cooker time	•	5 hours
finishing time	•	10–15 minutes
makes	•	4 servings

3 cups (750 mL) fish or chicken stock

3 Tbsp (45 mL) all-purpose flour

1 medium onion, diced

1 medium carrot, quartered lengthwise and sliced

1 large celery stalk, quartered lengthwise and sliced

1 garlic clove, minced

1¼ lb (625 g) salmon fillets, skinned and cubed

⅓ cup (80 mL) frozen peas

⅓ cup (80 mL) frozen corn kernels

2 tsp (10 mL) chopped fresh dill

Salt and white pepper to taste

ERIC'S OPTIONS
For a richer taste, swirl ⅓ cup (80 mL) of whipping cream into the stew just before adding the salmon. To make salmon and shrimp stew, reduce the amount of salmon added to the stew to 1 lb (500 g) and add ¼ lb (125 g) of cooked salad shrimp with the salmon.

Place the stock and flour in your slow cooker and whisk well until the flour is completely dissolved. Mix in the onion, carrot, celery and garlic. Cover and cook on the low setting for 5 hours, or until the vegetables are tender. Stir in the salmon, peas, corn, dill and salt and pepper. Cover and cook for 10 to 15 minutes more, or until the salmon is cooked through and the peas and corn are hot.

SNAPPER VERACRUZ-STYLE

This fish dish is named after the Mexican port city of Veracruz. Veracruz's cuisine was heavily influenced by the Spanish colonists and the ingredients, such as the olives and capers used in this recipe, they brought with them. What better to serve with this than Spanish-Style Brown Rice (page 186)?

28 oz (796 mL) can diced tomatoes

¾ cup (185 mL) fish or chicken stock

⅓ cup (80 mL) pimento-stuffed green olives, chopped

¼ cup (60 mL) finely chopped onion

¼ cup (60 mL) raisins

2 garlic cloves, minced

1 medium jalapeño pepper, seeded and finely chopped

2 Tbsp (30 mL) olive oil

2 Tbsp (30 mL) capers, drained

½ tsp (2.5 mL) dried oregano

Salt and freshly ground black pepper to taste

1½ lb (750 g) snapper fillets, cut into eight equal pieces

1 Tbsp (15 mL) chopped fresh parsley

preparation time	•	20 minutes
slow cooker time	•	4 hours
finishing time	•	15 minutes
makes	•	4 servings

ERIC'S OPTIONS
Instead of snapper, try bass, cod or halibut in this recipe. For added richness, drizzle servings of the fish with a little olive oil. Instead of parsley, you could sprinkle the fish with chopped fresh cilantro.

Set a sieve over a bowl. Drain the tomatoes into the sieve and reserve the juice. Use the back of a ladle to mash and coarsely crush the tomatoes.

Place the crushed tomatoes and the strained juice, and the stock, olives, onion, raisins, garlic, jalapeño pepper, oil, capers and oregano in your slow cooker and mix to combine. Cover and cook on the low setting for 4 hours. Season the sauce with salt and pepper. Nestle the fish partially into the sauce. Cover and cook for 15 minutes more, or until the fish is cooked through. Set 2 pieces of fish on each of 4 plates. Top the fish with the sauce, sprinkle with parsley and serve.

ABOUT SNAPPER AND ROCKFISH

You'll see snapper on restaurant menus and in supermarkets in various parts of the world. In warmer climates, snapper usually comes from a broad grouping of subtropical and tropical fish species. On the west coast of North America, though, the term "snapper" is also a market name for the rockfish commercially harvested off places such as Vancouver Island. There are a number of varieties of this fish, sometimes called Pacific snapper, but they are not related to the "true" Atlantic red snapper.

MEDITERRANEAN-STYLE SEAFOOD STEW

The base for this cioppino-like stew (pictured on page 177) is tastily accented with wine, garlic, basil and tomatoes. The fish, shrimp and crab are added about 20 minutes before you serve this dish. They cook fairly quickly and absorb the tasty base flavors. I like to serve this divine stew on a special occasion with crusty Italian bread and Roasted Red Pepper Aioli (page 176).

28 oz (796 mL) can whole tomatoes

1 cup (250 mL) fish or chicken stock

¾ cup (185 mL) dry white wine

1 medium onion, finely diced

1 small to medium green bell pepper, diced

2 garlic cloves, minced

2 Tbsp (30 mL) tomato paste

½ tsp (2.5 mL) dried oregano

¼ tsp (1 mL) dried thyme

Freshly ground black pepper to taste

16 large shrimp, peeled and deveined with tip of tail left intact (see Peeling and Deveining Shrimp on facing page)

¾ lb (375 g) cooked king crab legs (thawed if frozen), cut into 2-inch (5 cm) pieces

¾ lb (375 g) fresh snapper, halibut or cod fillet, cubed

1 Tbsp (15 mL) chopped fresh parsley

preparation time • 25 minutes
slow cooker time • 4 hours
finishing time • 18–22 minu
makes • 4 servings

ERIC'S OPTIONS
To spice up this stew, add crushed chili flakes to taste at the start of cooking. If you do not want to use wine, replace it with another ¾ cup (185 mL) of fish or chicken stock. The king crab could be replaced with an equal weight of cooked Dungeness or snow crab legs.

Drain the liquid from the canned tomatoes into your slow cooker. Coarsely chop the tomatoes and place them, along with any juices on the cutting board, in your slow cooker. Mix in the stock, wine, onion, bell pepper, garlic, tomato paste, oregano, thyme and black pepper. Cover and cook on the low setting for 4 hours, or until the vegetables are tender. Stir in the shrimp, crab and fish.

Cover, turn the heat to the high setting and cook for 10 minutes more.

Give the seafood a gentle stir and cook for 8 to 12 minutes more, or until the shrimp and fish are cooked and the crab is hot. Serve portions of the stew sprinkled with parsley.

PEELING AND DEVEINING SHRIMP

To peel a shrimp, grab its swimmerets (little legs), starting at the head end, and pull off the shell. You may need to do this in two or three steps, depending on the size of the shrimp.

Deveining removes the shrimp's dark intestinal vein. After peeling, take a sharp paring knife and make a shallow slit down the center of the flesh and pull out, or rinse out with cold water, the dark vein.

If peeling and deveining the shrimp sounds like a lot of work, many supermarkets now sell shrimp already peeled and deveined.

SHRIMP in PUTTANESCA SAUCE

Puttanesca sauce is a famous Italian tomato-based concoction boldly flavored with ingredients such as capers, olives and anchovies. "Puttanesca" comes from the Italian word *puttana*, which means prostitute. One story goes that this sauce, often served with pasta, was a quick and inexpensive meal for prostitutes to prepare, one that would also attract men to come visit because of its incredible aroma. You could serve this over plain, cooked pasta or flavored pasta, such as Spaghetti with Lemon, Chilies and Garlic (page 191).

preparation time • 20 minutes
slow cooker time • 4 hours
finishing time • 10 minutes
makes • 4 servings

2 cups (500 mL) strained tomatoes (see Note)

½ cup (125 mL) dry white wine or chicken or fish stock

½ cup (125 mL) pitted kalamata olives, coarsely chopped

4 anchovies, minced

2–3 garlic cloves, minced

2 Tbsp (30 mL) capers, drained well

2 Tbsp (30 mL) olive oil

Crushed chili flakes to taste

24 large shrimp, peeled and deveined with tip of tail left intact (see Peeling and Deveining Shrimp on page 59)

⅓ cup (80 mL) coarsely chopped fresh basil

NOTE
Bottled, strained tomatoes, also called *passata di pomodoro*, are tomatoes that have been cooked and then, as their name suggests, strained, giving them a rich tomato taste. They can be found in many supermarkets alongside the other tomato products. If you can't find strained tomatoes, you could use the same volume of tomato sauce in this recipe.

ERIC'S OPTIONS
Instead of anchovy fillets, you can use 2 tsp (10 mL) of anchovy paste in the sauce. Instead of basil, try another fresh herb in the sauce, such as fresh oregano or Italian parsley, or use a mix of herbs.

Place the tomatoes, wine or stock, olives, anchovies, garlic, capers, oil and chili flakes in your slow cooker and mix to combine. Cover and cook on the low setting for 4 hours.

Stir in the shrimp and cover and cook for 10 minutes more, or until the shrimp have turned a bright pink color and are just cooked through. Stir in the basil and serve.

SHRIMP in BEER and CHIPOTLE PEPPER BROTH

This tasty combination was inspired by a trip to the US Gulf Coast, where shrimp, beer and something spicy—in this case chipotle peppers—were often served together in one way or another. For a more filling meal, serve the shrimp with Spanish-Style Brown Rice (page 186).

preparation time	•	10 minutes
slow cooker time	•	4 hours
finishing time	•	10 minutes
makes	•	3–4 servings

1½ cups (375 mL) lager beer

1 cup (250 mL) chicken or vegetable stock

¼ cup (60 mL) fresh lime juice

1 medium onion, finely chopped

2 garlic cloves, minced

1–2 chipotle peppers, finely chopped (see Note)

1 Tbsp (15 mL) golden brown sugar

½ tsp (2.5 mL) ground cumin

24 large shrimp, peeled and deveined with tip of tail left intact (see Peeling and Deveining Shrimp on page 59)

¼ cup (60 mL) chopped fresh cilantro or sliced green onion

NOTE

Chipotle peppers are sold in cans in the Mexican food aisle of most supermarkets. Store the unused peppers in a tightly sealed jar in the refrigerator for several weeks.

ERIC'S OPTIONS

Replace the chipotle pepper—which is a smoked jalapeño pepper—with a large, fresh jalapeño, seeds removed and the flesh finely chopped. The broth will still be spicy, but won't have the smoky taste.

Combine the beer, stock, lime juice, onion, garlic, chipotle pepper, sugar and cumin in your slow cooker. Cover and cook on the low setting for 4 hours. Stir in the shrimp and cook for 10 minutes more, or until the shrimp have turned bright pink and are just cooked through.

Sprinkle servings of shrimp with chopped fresh cilantro or green onion.

RED THAI CURRY SHRIMP
and VEGETABLES

This silky, hard-to-resist coconut milk–based curry is chock-full of shrimp and vegetables. I like to serve it with steamed jasmine rice or Jasmine Fried Rice (page 180). You could also serve the curry with a palate-refreshing salad, such as Asian-Style Cucumber and Peanut Salad (page 170).

preparation time	•	25 minutes
slow cooker time	•	5 hours
finishing time	•	10 minutes
makes	•	4 servings

ERIC'S OPTIONS
This recipe calls for 1 Tbsp (15 mL) red Thai curry paste, which makes the dish mildly spicy. Feel free to double this amount, or add according to taste.

14 oz (398 mL) can regular or light coconut milk

1 cup (250 mL) chicken or fish stock

¼ cup (60 mL) fresh lime juice

3 Tbsp (45 mL) light soy sauce

1 Tbsp (15 mL) peeled, chopped fresh ginger (see About Fresh Ginger on page 30)

2 garlic cloves, chopped

3 Tbsp (45 mL) golden brown sugar

1 Tbsp (15 mL) cornstarch

1 Tbsp (15 mL) red Thai curry paste

1 medium onion, halved and thinly sliced

1 medium carrot, halved lengthwise, and thinly sliced on the bias

1 medium celery stalk, thinly sliced on the bias

1 medium red bell pepper, cut into small cubes

24 medium shrimp, peeled and deveined with tip of tail left intact (see Peeling and Deveining Shrimp on page 59)

¼ cup (60 mL) chopped fresh cilantro or thinly sliced green onion

Salt to taste

Place the coconut milk, stock, lime juice, soy sauce, ginger, garlic, brown sugar, cornstarch and curry paste in your slow cooker and whisk to thoroughly combine. Mix in the onion, carrot, celery and bell pepper. Cover and cook on the low setting for 5 hours, or until the vegetables are tender. Mix in the shrimp, cilantro and salt. Cover and cook for 10 minutes more, or until the shrimp are bright pink and just cooked through.

ABOUT THAI-STYLE CURRY PASTE

Thai-style curry pastes—green, red and yellow—are sold at Asian food stores and in the Asian food aisle of most supermarkets. They are named after the color of the chilies and other ingredients used to make them. I've used these pastes interchangeably in recipes, and what goes into them can vary from maker to maker, but generally speaking, green curry paste is the spiciest, red curry paste is a little less hot and yellow curry paste, which uses milder chilies, is the mildest.

SHRIMP GUMBO

The most important step in making this gumbo is cooking the roux—the oil and flour mixture that gives the gumbo its rich color. You must be patient, stirring and cooking it until it turns a chocolate-brown color. Don't leave the roux unattended as it cooks. The moment you take your eye off it it will inevitably burn and you'll have to make it again. Serve this with Cornbread with Pepper Jack Cheese (page 159).

⅓ cup (80 mL) vegetable oil

⅓ cup (80 mL) all-purpose flour

1 large onion, diced

2 medium celery stalks, diced

1 large green bell pepper, diced

2½ cups (625 mL) fish or chicken stock

14 oz (398 mL) can crushed tomatoes

2 tsp (10 mL) dried thyme

2 tsp (10 mL) hot pepper sauce, or to taste

1 bay leaf

1 Tbsp (15 mL) vegetable oil

10 fresh or frozen (thawed) whole okra, thinly sliced

24–36 medium to large shrimp, peeled and deveined with tip of tail left intact (see Peeling and Deveining Shrimp on page 59)

Salt and freshly ground black pepper to taste

2 cups (500 mL) cooked white rice, hot

2 green onions, thinly sliced

Continued . . .

preparation time	•	40 minutes
slow cooker time	•	6 hours
finishing time	•	10 minutes
makes	•	4 servings

ERIC'S OPTIONS

Make shrimp and crab gumbo by replacing 8 of the shrimp with 1 cup (250 mL) of fresh or frozen crabmeat, drained well. If you can't find fresh or frozen okra, you could use a 14 oz (398 mL) can of whole okra, drained well and sliced.

SHRIMP GUMBO
(*continued*)

Place the ⅓ cup (80 mL) of oil in a heavy-bottomed pot set over medium heat. When hot, add the flour and stir constantly until the roux (the oil/flour mixture) is a medium-brown color, 5 to 6 minutes. Mix in the onion and cook for 2 to 3 minutes. Add the celery and bell pepper and cook, stirring often, until the vegetables are softened and the roux is a chocolate-brown color, about 2 minutes more. Very, very slowly mix in the stock. Bring the mixture to a simmer, then pour into your slow cooker. Mix in the tomatoes, thyme, hot pepper sauce and bay leaf.

Heat the 1 Tbsp (15 mL) oil in a skillet set over medium-high heat. Add the okra and fry until golden, about 5 minutes. Mix the okra into the ingredients in the slow cooker. Cover and cook on the low setting for 6 hours, or until the vegetables are tender. Mix in the shrimp and salt and pepper. Cover and cook for 10 minutes more, or until the shrimp are bright pink and just cooked through.

Divide and mound the rice in the center of 4 large, shallow-sided bowls. Spoon the gumbo over or around the rice, sprinkle with green onion and serve.

LOBSTER TAILS with PROSCIUTTO, PESTO and TOMATOES

The sauce in which the split lobster tails are cooked sounds fancy, flavored as it is with the divine combination of pesto and prosciutto. However, it's actually easy to make, and takes only 10 minutes or less to get cooking in your slow cooker. I like to serve the lobster tails and sauce on a bed of pasta, such as linguini, with a salad alongside, such as Romaine Hearts with Focaccia Croutons and Parmesan (page 169).

28 oz (796 mL) can diced tomatoes

½ cup (125 mL) dry white wine

½ cup (125 mL) chicken, vegetable or fish stock

3 oz (90 g) prosciutto, diced

2 Tbsp (30 mL) tomato paste

1 Tbsp (15 mL) olive oil

2–3 Tbsp (30–45 mL) pesto

Freshly ground black pepper to taste

Eight 4–6 oz (125–175 g) lobster tails (thawed if frozen), split in half lengthwise

1 Tbsp (15 mL) chopped fresh parsley

preparation time	•	10 minutes*
slow cooker time	•	4 hours
finishing time	•	12–15 minutes
makes	•	3–4 servings

ERIC'S OPTIONS
Instead of prosciutto, cut 4 oz (125 g) of pancetta into small cubes, fry until crispy, drain and add to the tomato sauce mixture used to cook the lobster tails.

* more if thawing frozen lobster tails

Place the diced tomatoes, wine, stock, prosciutto, tomato paste and olive oil in your slow cooker. Cover and cook on the low setting for 4 hours. Stir in the pesto and pepper, then carefully set in the lobster tails, shell side down. Cover and cook for 12 to 15 minutes more, or until the lobster shells are reddish-pink and the meat is cooked through and just slightly firm. Sprinkle servings of the lobster with chopped fresh parsley.

POULTRY

DURBAN-STYLE CHICKEN CURRY

The South African city of Durban is famous for its red-hued curries, introduced to the area by Indian immigrants. This very tasty version is flavored with hot curry powder, and sweet paprika and crushed tomatoes give it a reddish color. Serve this with steamed basmati rice, warm wedges of naan bread and Fresh Mint Chutney (page 173).

3 Tbsp (45 mL) vegetable oil

8 chicken thighs

½ tsp (2.5 mL) sweet paprika (see About Paprika on facing page)

Salt and freshly ground black pepper to taste

1 medium onion, diced

1 garlic clove, minced

1 Tbsp (15 mL) peeled, chopped fresh ginger (see About Fresh Ginger on page 30)

1–2 Tbsp (15–30 mL) hot curry powder

14 oz (398 mL) can crushed tomatoes

14 oz (398 mL) can regular or light coconut milk

1 Tbsp (15 mL) golden brown sugar

2 Tbsp (30 mL) fresh lime juice

1 Tbsp (15 mL) cornstarch

2 Tbsp (30 mL) chopped fresh cilantro or sliced green onion

Place the oil in a large skillet set over medium-high heat. Sprinkle and rub the chicken with the paprika and salt and pepper. Brown the thighs on both sides and place in your slow cooker. Drain off most of the fat from the skillet, add the onion, garlic and ginger and cook for 2 to 3 minutes. Mix in the curry powder and cook for 1 minute more. Mix in the crushed tomatoes, coconut milk and brown sugar. Combine the lime juice and

preparation time • 25 minutes
slow cooker time • 6 hours
makes • 4 servings

ERIC'S OPTIONS
For a milder curry, use mild or medium curry powder instead of the hot.

cornstarch in a small bowl to dissolve the cornstarch. Stir this into the coconut milk mixture, bring to a simmer and pour over the chicken. Cover and cook on the low setting for 6 hours, or until the chicken is very tender. Sprinkle servings of the chicken with cilantro or green onion.

ABOUT PAPRIKA

Paprika is a spice made from dried, ground, sweet red pepper pods. Although there are several types, the spice is divided into two main varieties, sweet paprika and hot paprika. Hot paprika is made from peppers that have some heat to them. Supermarkets usually sell the sweeter varieties of paprika in containers that are generically labeled "paprika," not "sweet paprika." Tins or jars of hot paprika will be labeled "hot." Smoking the peppers before they are dried and ground creates a spice called smoked paprika. You'll find smoked paprika at fine food stores and some supermarkets.

CHICKEN in SOUR CREAM PAPRIKA SAUCE

In this dish, chicken is cooked in a paprika-rich sauce until it is deliciously tender. Serve the chicken with egg noodles and a green vegetable to add color to the plate. Broccoli with Lemon Zest, Ginger and Red Pepper (pictured; recipe page 210) is perfect with this.

preparation time	•	20 minutes
slow cooker time	•	6 hours
finishing time	•	15 minutes
makes	•	4–6 serving

ERIC'S OPTIONS
For a smoky paprika taste, replace 2 tsp (10 mL) of the regular sweet paprika with smoked paprika.

6 chicken drumsticks

6 chicken thighs

Salt and freshly ground black pepper to taste

2 small to medium onions, halved and sliced

2 small to medium celery stalks, halved lengthwise and sliced

2 small to medium carrots, halved lengthwise and sliced

2 garlic cloves, minced

2½ cups (625 mL) chicken stock

3 Tbsp (45 mL) all-purpose flour

2 Tbsp (30 mL) sweet paprika (see About Paprika on page 71)

1 tsp (5 mL) ground marjoram

½ cup (125 mL) regular or low-fat sour cream

½ cup (125 mL) frozen peas

Chopped fresh parsley to taste

Set an oven rack 6 inches (15 cm) below the broiler. Preheat the broiler to high.

Set the chicken on a nonstick baking sheet and season with salt and pepper. Broil the chicken until lightly browned, 4 to 5 minutes per side. Remove the chicken from the oven.

Continued . . .

CHICKEN in SOUR CREAM PAPRIKA SAUCE
(*continued*)

Place the onions, celery, carrots and garlic in your slow cooker and mix to combine. Nestle the chicken into the vegetables. Place the stock, flour, paprika and marjoram in a bowl and whisk to combine. Pour this mixture over the chicken. Cover and cook on the low setting for 6 hours, or until the chicken is very tender.

Preheat the oven to 200°F (95°C).

Carefully lift the chicken out of the slow cooker and set in a 13- × 19-inch (3.5 L) serving casserole. Keep the chicken warm in the oven. Ladle ½ cup (125 mL) of the sauce from the slow cooker into a small bowl and whisk in the sour cream. Add this mixture to the remaining sauce and vegetables in the slow cooker and mix well to combine. Stir in the peas, cover and cook for 10 minutes more to heat the sour cream and peas through. Season to taste with salt and pepper. Pour the mixture over the chicken, sprinkle with parsley and serve.

CHICKEN and VEGETABLE STEW

This no-fuss stew involves slow-simmering cubes of chicken and a mix of vegetables with stock and flavorings in your slow cooker. Light cream adds richness, and quick-to-heat frozen peas and corn add flavor and color. This stew tastes even better when served over Whipped Yukon Gold Potatoes (page 200). You could also serve it with Buttermilk Biscuits (page 156).

preparation time	•	20 minutes
slow cooker time	•	6 hours
finishing time	•	10 minutes
makes	•	4 servings

ERIC'S OPTIONS
If you don't want to use cream, add an extra ⅓ cup (80 mL) of stock at the beginning of cooking. Instead of sage, try another dried herb, such as tarragon or thyme.

2½ cups (625 mL) chicken stock

¼ cup (60 mL) all-purpose flour

1¼ lb (625 g) boneless, skinless chicken breast or thigh, cubed

2 medium carrots, halved lengthwise and sliced

2 medium celery stalks, halved lengthwise and sliced

2 garlic cloves, minced

1 medium onion, diced

1 tsp (5 mL) dried sage leaves (see Note on page 46)

⅓ cup (80 mL) light (10%) cream

⅓ cup (80 mL) frozen peas

⅓ cup (80 mL) frozen corn kernels

Salt and freshly ground black pepper to taste

1 Tbsp (15 mL) chopped fresh parsley

Place the stock and flour in your slow cooker. Whisk until the flour is completely dissolved. Mix in the chicken, carrots, celery, garlic, onion and sage. Cover and cook on the low setting for 6 hours, or until the chicken and vegetables are tender. Stir in the cream, peas, corn and salt and pepper, cover and cook for another 10 minutes, or until the peas and corn are heated through. Sprinkle servings of the chicken with chopped fresh parsley.

Also pictured: Mango Chutney (page 178) and Jasmine Fried Rice (page 180).

GREEN THAI CURRY CHICKEN THIGHS

This is my version of the green Thai chicken curry offered in just about every Thai restaurant in the world. Serve this saucy chicken with steamed jasmine rice or Jasmine Fried Rice (page 180), and Mango Chutney (page 178).

preparation time • 20 minutes
slow cooker time • 5–6 hours
makes • 4 servings

Two 14 oz (398 mL) cans regular or light coconut milk

3 Tbsp (45 mL) fresh lime juice

1–2 Tbsp (15–30 mL) green Thai curry paste

1 Tbsp (15 mL) cornstarch

1 Tbsp (15 mL) light soy sauce

1 Tbsp (15 mL) honey

8 boneless, skinless chicken thighs, sliced in ¼-inch (6 mm) wide strips

14 oz (398 mL) can cut miniature (baby) corn, drained well

7½ oz (213 mL) can sliced water chestnuts, drained well

1 medium red onion, halved and thinly sliced

1 medium carrot, halved lengthwise and sliced on the bias

1 Tbsp (15 mL) peeled, chopped fresh ginger (see About Fresh Ginger on page 30)

¼ cup (60 mL) chopped fresh cilantro or sliced green onion

Place the coconut milk, lime juice, curry paste, cornstarch, soy sauce and honey in your slow cooker and whisk to combine. Mix in the chicken, corn, water chestnuts, onion, carrot and ginger. Cover and cook on the low setting for 5 to 6 hours, or until the chicken is tender. Swirl in the chopped cilantro or sliced green onions and serve.

CHICKEN BREAST COQ AU VIN

This version of the famous wine-laced French dish uses boneless, skinless chicken breast cubes instead of the traditional bone-in pieces of chicken. This means you can eat the chicken with only a fork, which makes this dish ideal for a potluck party where table seating is limited and some folks are eating out of their laps. Serve this with a side dish that will tastily soak up its sauce, such as Saffron Rice with Parsley (page 185) or Mixed Vegetable Rice Pilaf (page 184).

2½ lb (1.25 kg) boneless, skinless chicken breast, cut in 1½ inch (4 cm) cubes

Salt and freshly ground black pepper to taste

¼ cup (60 mL) all-purpose flour

3 Tbsp (45 mL) olive oil

4 thick slices bacon, diced

1 lb (500 g) white or brown mushrooms, quartered (see Buying and Storing White and Brown Mushrooms on page 121)

2 garlic cloves, minced

1 large onion, diced

1 cup (250 mL) red wine

1½ cups (375 mL) chicken stock

2 tsp (10 mL) herbes de Provence (see Note on page 8)

preparation time • 40 minutes
slow cooker time • 6 hours
makes • 8 servings

ERIC'S OPTIONS
If you want to use white and dark chicken meat, replace half the chicken breast with boneless, skinless chicken thigh. For a more exotic mushroom taste, use a mix of mushrooms, such as oyster, shiitake and white or brown mushrooms.

Place the chicken in a bowl, season with salt and pepper and coat with the flour. Place the oil in a large skillet set over medium-high heat. When hot, brown the chicken in batches, setting the cooked pieces in your slow cooker as you go. Reserve any flour left in the bowl.

Add the bacon to the skillet and cook until crisp. Add the mushrooms, garlic and onion and cook for 5 minutes. Mix in any flour left in the bowl. Slowly mix in the wine. Stir in the stock and herbes de Provence and bring to a simmer. Pour this mixture over the chicken. Cover and cook on the low setting for 6 hours, or until the chicken is tender. Adjust the seasoning, adding more salt and pepper if needed.

ABOUT COQ AU VIN

Coq au vin translates as "rooster with wine." The dish is sometimes considered a contemporary French creation, but its roots can be traced back to that country's long-standing rural tradition of tenderizing tough meat—such as an old rooster—by slowly simmering it for hours in a casserole with wine and/or broth. Nowadays, the dish is most often made with a young chicken, not an old one, and is well suited for the slow cooker's low-temperature environs.

I love to serve coq au vin on festive occasions in the wintertime, when a simmering casserole of chicken, wine, mushrooms, onions and bits of bacon can provide a merry way to take the chill out of even the coldest day.

CHICKEN BREAST CACCIATORE

Cacciatore is Italian for "hunter." The term became associated with this dish because hunters supplied the game used to make it. In modern culinary lingo, it refers to a meat or poultry stew accented with such things as tomatoes, onions and herbs. I like to serve the chicken with plain cooked pasta, or flavored pasta such as Orzo with Basil and Parmesan Cheese (page 192). Roasted Garlic Bread (page 154) would also go nicely with the chicken.

1¼ lb (625 g) boneless, skinless chicken breast, cubed

2 cups (500 mL) tomato basil pasta sauce (see Note)

1 cup (250 mL) red wine or chicken stock

½ cup (125 mL) pimento-stuffed green olives, sliced

2 garlic cloves, minced

1 medium onion, diced

1 medium green bell pepper, diced

1 medium carrot, halved lengthwise and sliced

Salt and freshly ground black pepper to taste

1 Tbsp (15 mL) chopped fresh parsley

preparation time	•	20 minutes
slow cooker time	•	6 hours
makes	•	4 servings

NOTE
Tomato basil pasta sauce is available in the bottled and canned tomato products aisle of most supermarkets.

ERIC'S OPTIONS
If you prefer dark chicken meat, use boneless, skinless chicken thighs instead of the chicken breast. If you prefer black olives, use those instead of the green olives. For a spicy taste, mix in a few pinches of crushed chili flakes at the start of cooking.

Place the chicken, pasta sauce, wine, olives, garlic, onion, bell pepper and carrot in your slow cooker and mix to combine. Cover and cook on the low setting for 6 hours, or until the chicken is tender. Taste and, if necessary, season the cacciatore with salt and pepper. Sprinkle servings of the chicken with chopped fresh parsley.

ABOUT PARSLEY

Parsley is an underrated herb that attracted an undeserved reputation for being run-of-the-mill. However, chefs seem to be rediscovering its value. And why not? A little of it freshly chopped and mixed into, or sprinkled over, soups, stews, casseroles, poached fish and many other dishes will instantly add flavor and appearance.

The two main types of parsley are curly leaf parsley and flat-leaf (also called Italian) parsley. You can easily tell the two apart from the shape of the leaves. There is not a great difference in taste between the two; both are described as very slightly peppery and palate refreshing.

To store parsley, wrap it in a slightly dampened paper towel, set it in a plastic bag and refrigerate for up to a week. Parsley needs to be washed well just before using as its leaves are prone to collecting dirt.

Parsley is so much more than a pretty garnish. It contains vitamins A and C as well as calcium and iron.

CHICKEN WINGS with BOURBON, MAPLE and CITRUS

Finger-licking-good wings jacked up with bourbon, the famous American whiskey named for Bourbon County, Kentucky. Its taste, slightly smoky with a hint of molasses, makes it a good ingredient to blend into barbecue sauce. Serve the wings as a snack or make a southern-style meal by serving them with Spanish-Style Brown Rice (pictured; recipe page 186) and Green Beans with Pecans, Lime and Honey (page 212).

1¼ cups (310 mL) barbecue sauce

½ cup (125 mL) bourbon

½ cup (125 mL) orange juice

¼ cup (60 mL) maple syrup

2 Tbsp (30 mL) fresh lime juice

18 chicken wingettes (see Note on page 84)

18 chicken drumettes (see Note on page 84)

2 Tbsp (30 mL) vegetable oil

1 Tbsp (15 mL) Cajun spice (see Note), or to taste

½ tsp (2.5 mL) salt (see Note)

preparation time	•	15 minutes
slow cooker time	•	3–4 hours
makes	•	4–6 servings

NOTE

Cajun spice is a Louisiana-style blend of herbs and spices. You will find it in the bottled herb and spice aisle of most supermarkets. Some producers add salt to the mix. In that case, omit the ½ tsp (2.5 mL) salt.

ERIC'S OPTIONS

The spiciness of Cajun spice varies between brands. It's a good idea to place a tiny amount on the tip of your finger and taste it. If it's mild and you like things spicy, add a little more Cajun spice than the amount listed here.

Place the barbecue sauce, bourbon, orange juice, maple syrup and lime juice in your slow cooker and whisk to combine.

Set an oven rack 6 inches (15 cm) below the broiler. Preheat the broiler to high.

Place the chicken, oil, Cajun spice and salt in a bowl and toss to combine. Arrange the chicken in a single layer on a nonstick baking sheet. Broil for 4 to 5 minutes per side, or until nicely browned. Add the chicken to the slow cooker and stir to coat with the sauce. Cover and cook on the high setting for 3 to 4 hours, or until tender. Arrange the wingettes and drumettes on a platter or on plates. Skim off any fat from the surface of the sauce and serve it in a bowl alongside for dipping or drizzling overtop.

SWEET and TANGY BARBECUE WINGS

The sweet in these wings (pictured in the background on page 205) comes from honey; fresh lime juice provides the tang. Add your favorite barbecue sauce, beer, garlic and spices and you will end up with wings so tasty they'll fly off the plate. Serve the wings as a snack or make a meal of them by serving them with a green salad and Broccoli and Cheddar–Stuffed Potatoes (page 204).

1¾ cups (435 mL) barbecue sauce

¾ cup (185 mL) lager beer

¼ cup (60 mL) honey

¼ cup (60 mL) fresh lime juice

2 garlic cloves, minced

1 Tbsp (15 mL) hot pepper sauce, such as Tabasco

18 chicken drumettes (see Note)

18 chicken wingettes (see Note)

2 Tbsp (30 mL) vegetable oil

1 tsp (5 mL) ground cumin

½ tsp (2.5 mL) sweet paprika (see About Paprika on page 71)

Salt and freshly ground black pepper to taste

preparation time	•	15 minutes
slow cooker time	•	3–4 hours
makes	•	4–6 serving

NOTE

Wingettes are the flat, middle portion of the wing and drumettes are the meaty section attached to the breast. If your store does not sell them this way, you'll have to buy whole wings and split them yourself. This is easier than you might think. You simply cut them in half where the wingette and drumette meet.

ERIC'S OPTIONS

If you don't want to use alcohol, replace the beer with chicken stock. For added flavor and color, sprinkle the wings with chopped fresh cilantro or sliced green onion before serving.

Place the barbecue sauce, beer, honey, lime juice, garlic and hot pepper sauce in your slow cooker and whisk to combine.

Set an oven rack 6 inches (15 cm) below the broiler. Preheat the broiler to high.

Place the chicken, oil, cumin, paprika and salt and pepper in a bowl and toss to combine. Arrange the chicken in a single layer on a nonstick baking sheet. Broil for 4 to 5 minutes per side, or until nicely browned. Add the chicken to the slow cooker and stir to coat with the sauce. Cover and cook on the high setting for 3 to 4 hours, or until the chicken is tender. Arrange the wingettes and drumettes on a platter or on plates. Skim any fat from the surface of the sauce and serve it in a bowl alongside for dipping or drizzling overtop.

TURKEY MEATBALLS
in ONION GRAVY

Lean ground turkey is flavored with garlic and sage, rolled into balls, roasted and slowly simmered in a simple sauce. Serve the meatballs with egg noodles and Brussels Sprouts with Apples and Walnuts (page 216).

preparation time	•	35 minutes
slow cooker time	•	6 hours
finishing time	•	5 minutes
makes	•	4–6 servings

1¼ lb (625 g) lean ground turkey

⅓ cup (80 mL) dried breadcrumbs

2 Tbsp (30 mL) milk

1 large garlic clove, minced

1 large egg, beaten

1 tsp (5 mL) dried sage leaves (see Note on page 46)

½ tsp (2.5 mL) salt

Freshly ground black pepper to taste

3 cups (750 mL) chicken stock

¼ cup (60 mL) all-purpose flour

1 medium onion, diced

¼ cup (60 mL) regular or low-fat sour cream

2 green onions, thinly sliced

ERIC'S OPTIONS
Instead of ground turkey, try using another type of ground meat, such as beef or veal. If you don't want to use dairy in this recipe, simply omit the milk and sour cream and increase the amount of stock used to 3¼ cups (810 mL). The meatballs won't taste as rich, but they will still be good.

Preheat the oven to 375°F (190°C). Line a baking sheet with parchment paper.

Place the turkey, breadcrumbs, milk, garlic, egg, sage and salt and pepper in a bowl and mix to combine. Moisten your hands with cold water. Roll the meat mixture into 1½-inch (4 cm) balls and set on the baking sheet. Roast for 20 minutes, or until cooked through.

Place the stock and flour in your slow cooker and whisk until the flour is completely dissolved. Mix in the diced onion and add the meatballs. Cover and cook on the low setting for 6 hours, or until the meatballs are tender. With a slotted spoon, scoop the meatballs out of the sauce and into a serving dish. Whisk the sour cream into the sauce in the slow cooker and warm through. Spoon the sauce over the meatballs, sprinkle with green onion and serve.

SWEET-and-SOUR TURKEY MEATBALLS

Tender, Asian-style meatballs are simmered with bits of green bell pepper and golden chunks of pineapple. Serve the meatballs on steamed rice or Cashew Fried Rice (page 182).

1 lb (500 g) lean ground turkey

¼ cup (60 mL) dried breadcrumbs

1 large egg, beaten

2 tsp (10 mL) peeled, grated fresh ginger (see About Fresh Ginger on page 30)

1 garlic clove, minced

½ tsp (2.5 mL) salt

Freshly ground black pepper to taste

14 oz (398 mL) can tomato sauce

¼ cup (60 mL) ketchup

¼ cup (60 mL) rice vinegar

3 Tbsp (45 mL) honey

1 Tbsp (15 mL) soy sauce

2 tsp (10 mL) cornstarch

19 oz (540 mL) can unsweetened pineapple chunks

1 medium green bell pepper, diced

2 green onions, thinly sliced

Continued . . .

preparation time	•	35 minutes
slow cooker time	•	6 hours
makes	•	4–6 servings

ERIC'S OPTIONS
Make sweet, sour and spicy meatballs by adding hot Asian-style chili sauce, to taste, when blending the tomato sauce and other liquid ingredients together.

SWEET-and-SOUR TURKEY MEATBALLS
(*continued*)

Preheat the oven to 375°F (190°C). Line a baking sheet with parchment paper.

Place the turkey, breadcrumbs, egg, ginger, garlic, salt and pepper in a bowl and mix to combine. Moisten your hands with cold water. Roll the meat mixture into 1½-inch (4 cm) balls and set on the prepared baking sheet. Roast for 20 minutes, or until cooked through.

Place the tomato sauce, ketchup, vinegar, honey, soy sauce and cornstarch in your slow cooker and whisk to combine. Add the meatballs, pineapple (fruit and juice) and bell pepper and gently swirl to combine. Cover and cook on the low setting for 6 hours, or until the meatballs are tender. Sprinkle servings of the meatballs with green onion.

TEX-MEX
TURKEY CHILI

Tex-Mex is a culinary term that originated in Texas. It evolved as a way of describing the fusion of foods available in the Southwest with techniques and culinary traditions Mexican immigrants brought to the area. Serve this with Cornbread with Pepper Jack Cheese (page 159).

preparation time • **25 minutes**
slow cooker time • **8 hours**
makes • **8 servings**

(page 159).

ERIC'S OPTIONS
Instead of ground turkey, try using another type of ground meat in this recipe, such as beef or pork. Dress up bowls of this chili by topping them with a dollop of sour cream and some grated Monterey Jack or cheddar cheese.

1½ lb (750 g) lean ground turkey

28 oz (796 mL) can crushed tomatoes

28 oz (796 mL) can diced tomatoes

19 oz (540 mL) can black beans, drained, rinsed in cold water and drained again

19 oz (540 mL) can pinto beans, drained, rinsed in cold water and drained again

1 cup (250 mL) frozen corn kernels

1 cup (250 mL) lager beer or chicken stock

1 medium onion, diced

1 medium green bell pepper, diced

1–2 tsp (5–10 mL) hot pepper sauce

2 tsp (10 mL) chili powder

1 tsp (5 mL) ground cumin

1 tsp (5 mL) dried oregano

Salt and freshly ground black pepper to taste

¼ cup (60 mL) chopped fresh cilantro (optional)

Place the turkey in a nonstick skillet and set over medium heat. Stir and cook the turkey until completely cooked through and crumbly, then drain off any excess liquid. Spoon the turkey into your slow cooker. Mix in the crushed and diced tomatoes, canned beans, corn, beer, onion, bell pepper, hot pepper sauce, chili powder, cumin and oregano. Cover and cook on the low setting for 8 hours, or until bubbly and delicious. Stir in the salt, pepper and cilantro, if using, and serve.

SAVOY CABBAGE ROLLS with TURKEY, ONION and SAGE

I like to use savoy cabbage to make cabbage rolls. The leaves come off the head more easily than tightly wound green cabbage leaves do and their frilly appearance makes the cabbage rolls look more attractive on the plate. Serve these with slices of dense rye bread and store-bought or homemade pickled beets, such as Pickled Beets with Balsamic and Spice (pictured; recipe page 174).

1 lb (500 g) lean ground turkey

1½ cups (375 mL) cooked long-grain white rice, cold

1 large egg, beaten

½ medium onion, finely diced

2 garlic cloves, minced

1 tsp (5 mL) dried sage leaves (see Note on page 46)

1 tsp (5 mL) salt

½ tsp (2.5 mL) freshly ground black pepper

8 savoy cabbage leaves, each about 5 inches (12 cm) wide

1 medium onion, halved and thinly sliced

2 cups (500 mL) tomato sauce

1½ cups (375 mL) chicken stock

1 Tbsp (15 mL) all-purpose flour

1 Tbsp (15 mL) honey

1 Tbsp (15 mL) balsamic vinegar

1 Tbsp (15 mL) chopped fresh parsley

Continued . . .

preparation time ●	**40 minutes**
slow cooker time ●	**6 hours**
makes ●	**4 servings***

ERIC'S OPTIONS
Instead of ground turkey, use ground beef in this recipe. For added fiber, use the same volume of cold, cooked long-grain brown rice instead of white rice.

* 2 cabbage rolls each

SAVOY CABBAGE ROLLS with TURKEY, ONION and SAGE (*continued*)

Place the turkey, rice, egg, diced onion, garlic, sage, salt and pepper in a bowl and mix to combine.

Bring a large pot of water to a boil. Add the cabbage to the boiling water and cook until just tender, 2 to 3 minutes. Cool the cabbage in ice-cold water and drain well. Trim off the tough, lower part of the vein running through the center of each leaf and discard.

Spread half of the sliced onion over the bottom of your slow cooker. Set the cabbage leaves, curved side down, on a work surface. Spoon an equal amount of the rice mixture into the center of each cabbage leaf. Fold the sides of each cabbage leaf over the filling and tightly roll. Set the cabbage rolls, seam side down, in your slow cooker.

Place the tomato sauce, stock, flour, honey and vinegar in a bowl and whisk to combine. Pour over the cabbage rolls, then sprinkle with the remaining onion slices. Cook on the low setting for 6 hours, or until the cabbage rolls are tender. Set 2 cabbage rolls on each plate. Spoon over the sauce from the slow cooker, sprinkle with parsley and enjoy.

SLOW-SIMMERED FRENCH-STYLE BEANS with CONFIT DUCK LEG

The beans in this recipe are gently simmered in your slow cooker with French-style accents, such as the aromatic herb blend herbes de Provence. When the beans are almost done, confit duck legs are roasted in a hot oven until their skins are crispy. To serve, the beans are spooned into shallow bowls and duck legs set on top (pictured on page 165). I like to serve a salad before or alongside this dish. Butter Lettuce Salad with Walnuts and Dried Cherries (page 164) works well.

2 cups (500 mL) dried small white or navy beans

2 cups (500 mL) chicken stock

1 cup (250 mL) dry white wine

3 Tbsp (45 mL) olive oil

1 medium onion, diced

1 large carrot, diced

2 garlic cloves, minced

1 tsp (5 mL) herbes de Provence (see Note on page 8)

2 bay leaves

6 confit duck legs (see Note)

Salt and freshly ground black pepper to taste

2 Tbsp (30 mL) chopped fresh parsley

preparation time •	45 minutes
slow cooker time •	6 hours*
makes •	6 servings

NOTE
Ready-to-roast confit duck legs are available at some fine food stores, delis and butcher shops.

ERIC'S OPTIONS
If you can't find, or don't want to use, confit duck legs, which are slowly simmered in duck fat and flavorings, you could replace them with 6 grilled or roasted fresh sausages, such as andouille, chorizo or country-style.

* includes 35 minutes to roast the duck

Place the beans in a large pot and cover with 10 cups (2.5 L) of cold water. Bring to a boil, then reduce the heat until the water is gently simmering. Cook the beans until just tender, about 45 minutes. Drain the beans well and place in your slow cooker. Mix in the stock, wine, oil, onion, carrot, garlic, herbes de Provence and bay leaves. Cover and cook on the low setting for 6 hours.

Continued . . .

SLOW-SIMMERED FRENCH-STYLE BEANS
with CONFIT DUCK LEG (*continued*)

After 5 hours 15 minutes' cooking time, preheat your oven to 425°F (220°C). Line a large, shallow-sided roasting pan with parchment paper.

Remove the excess fat from the outside of each duck leg. Set the duck, skin side up, in the roasting pan. Roast for 35 minutes, or until the skin is crisp and golden.

When the beans are done, season with salt and pepper. Divide the beans among 6 shallow-sided bowls. Top each bowl of beans with a duck leg. Sprinkle with parsley and serve.

PORK

PORK ROAST in MAPLE WHISKEY SAUCE

As the pork slowly cooks and becomes very tender, it will be divinely flavored with the bold taste of whiskey, the sweetness of maple syrup, the tanginess of cider vinegar and a hint of spicy Dijon mustard. Create a tasty meal by serving this with Boiled, Smashed and Fried New Potatoes (page 201) and Broccoli with Lemon Zest, Ginger and Red Pepper (page 210).

preparation time • **25 minutes**
slow cooker time • **7–8 hours**
finishing time • **15 minutes**
makes • **6 servings**

ERIC'S OPTIONS
Make maple rum sauce by replacing the whiskey with an equal amount of dark rum. Make honey whiskey sauce by replacing the maple syrup with an equal amount of honey.

2 Tbsp (30 mL) vegetable oil

3 lb (1.5 kg) boneless pork loin or leg roast

Salt and freshly ground black pepper to taste

2 medium onions, halved and sliced

¾ **cup (185 mL)** Canadian or bourbon whiskey

½ **cup (125 mL)** chicken stock

¼ **cup (60 mL)** maple syrup

3 Tbsp (45 mL) cider vinegar

2 Tbsp (30 mL) Dijon mustard

1 Tbsp (15 mL) cornstarch

1 tsp (5 mL) dried sage leaves (see Note on page 46)

Place the oil in a large skillet set over medium-high heat. Season the pork with salt and pepper. When the oil is hot, add the pork to the skillet and sear it on all sides. Place the pork in your slow cooker. Add the onions to the skillet and sauté until tender, about 5 minutes. Place the remaining ingredients in a bowl and whisk to combine. Stir this mixture into the onions, bring to a simmer and pour over the pork. Cover and cook on the low setting for 7 to 8 hours, or until the pork is very tender.

To serve, remove the pork from the sauce and set on a plate. Tent with foil and rest for 10 minutes. Skim off any fat from the sauce. Taste the sauce and season with salt and pepper, if needed. Slice the pork, plate and top with the sauce.

PORK SHOULDER ROAST with WINE, OLIVES and TOMATOES

This dish is like pot roast, except that it is made with pork, not beef. It is richly flavored Italian-style. Serve slices of this with steamed rapini or broccoli and Orzo with Basil and Parmesan Cheese (page 192). When cooked, a fair amount of sauce will surround the pork, and that's a good thing. Any remaining sauce and meat, diced, can be heated together in a skillet and served over hot pasta, creating another meal you can serve a day or two later.

2 Tbsp (30 mL) olive oil

2¾ lb (1.375 kg) boneless pork shoulder (butt) roast

Salt and freshly ground black pepper to taste

1 cup (250 mL) red wine

¼ cup (60 mL) all-purpose flour

2 Tbsp (30 mL) tomato paste

28 oz (796 mL) can diced tomatoes

1 medium onion, halved and thinly sliced

1 medium green bell pepper, cubed

¾ cup (185 mL) pimento-stuffed green olives, sliced

2 garlic cloves, minced

1 Tbsp (15 mL) honey

2 tsp (10 mL) dried oregano

2 Tbsp (30 mL) chopped fresh parsley

preparation time	• 20 minutes
slow cooker time	• 8 hours
finishing time	• 15 minutes
makes	• 6 servings

ERIC'S OPTIONS

If you're a fan of garlic, instead of mixing 2 minced garlic cloves into the sauce for the pork, stud the pork roast with garlic slices before browning. Simply take a long, narrow knife and make numerous deep slits into the meat. Push thickly sliced pieces of garlic deep into the slits so you can no longer see them.

Place the oil in a skillet set over medium-high heat. Season the pork with salt and pepper. When the oil is hot, brown the pork on all sides.

Place the wine, flour and tomato paste in your slow cooker and whisk until the flour is completely dissolved. Add the diced tomatoes, onion, bell pepper, olives, garlic, honey and oregano and mix to combine. Set the pork in the slow cooker, turning to coat with the sauce. Cover and cook on the low setting for 8 hours, or until the pork is very tender.

Remove the pork from the sauce and set on a plate. Tent with foil and let rest for 10 minutes. Skim off any fat from the sauce. Taste the sauce and season with salt and pepper, if needed. Slice the pork, plate and top with sauce. Sprinkle with parsley and serve.

ABOUT PORK SHOULDER ROAST AND STEAK

Budget-friendly pork shoulder roast and steak, also known as pork butt roast and steak, are cut from the top portion of the front shoulder of the pig. Pork shoulder roast and steak have a higher fat content than leaner cuts of pork, such as the loin. That fat enhances the flavor of the meat, which becomes quite succulent when slowly cooked, whether in a barbecue pit or in a slow cooker.

BONELESS PORK CHOPS with APPLES, ONIONS and SAGE

Pork and apples always taste great together. You can enhance their harmonious flavors by serving this dish with boiled new potatoes and Candied Carrots and Parsnips with Peas (pictured; recipe page 213).

preparation time • 20 minutes
slow cooker time • 6–7 hours
makes • 4 servings*

3 medium apples, peeled, halved, cored and sliced

2 Tbsp (30 mL) fresh lemon juice

2 medium onions, halved and thinly sliced

2 tsp (10 mL) dried sage leaves (see Note on page 46)

Salt and freshly ground black pepper to taste

3 Tbsp (45 mL) vegetable oil

Eight 3 oz (90 g) boneless pork loin chops

⅓ cup (80 mL) all-purpose flour

1 cup (250 mL) chicken stock

¾ cup (185 mL) unsweetened apple juice

ERIC'S OPTIONS
Instead of boneless pork chops, use 4 large bone-in pork chops in this recipe. For an alcoholic apple taste, replace ¼ to ½ cup (60 to 125 mL) of the apple juice with apple brandy.

* 2 chops each

Combine the apples and lemon juice in a large bowl. Toss in the onions, sage and salt and pepper. Spoon half the mixture into your slow cooker.

Place the oil in a large skillet set over medium-high heat. Season the pork with salt and pepper, then dredge it in the flour, shaking off any excess. Brown the pork chops on both sides. Set the pork chops on top of the apple/onion mixture in your slow cooker. Top the chops with the remaining apple/onion mixture in the bowl. Pour the stock and apple juice into the slow cooker. Cover and cook on the low setting for 6 to 7 hours, or until the pork is tender.

PORK CHOPS with APRICOTS and CABBAGE

This recipe is like a meat entrée and side dish all in one. The tender pork chops are the entrée; the earthy cabbage, slow-cooked underneath the chops and accented with sliced apricots and onions, is the side dish. Put them on the plate together and serve up another side dish, such as Boiled, Smashed and Fried New Potatoes (pictured; recipe page 201), and you'll have a very inviting meal to enjoy.

5 cups (1.25 L) coarsely chopped green cabbage

12 dried apricots, each halved lengthwise

1 medium onion, halved and thinly sliced

2 Tbsp (30 mL) vegetable oil

Four 7 oz (200 g) pork chops

Salt and freshly ground black pepper to taste

2 cups (500 mL) chicken stock

¼ cup (60 mL) all-purpose flour

½ cup (125 mL) orange juice

1 large garlic clove, minced

1 tsp (5 mL) dried sage leaves (see Note on page 46)

preparation time	•	25 minutes
slow cooker time	•	6–7 hours
makes	•	4 servings

ERIC'S OPTIONS

For a different dried fruit taste, sprinkle ⅓ cup (80 mL) dried cranberries onto the cabbage in the bottom of your slow cooker. Instead of bone-in pork chops, try using eight 3 oz (90 g) boneless pork loin chops.

Spread the cabbage in the bottom of your slow cooker and sprinkle the apricots and onion overtop. Place the oil in a large skillet set over medium-high heat. When the oil is hot, season the chops with salt and pepper, brown on both sides and set on top of the cabbage. Drain any fat from the skillet and set it back over medium-high heat.

Place the stock in a bowl and whisk in the flour until lump-free. Mix in the orange juice, garlic and sage. Pour this mixture into the skillet, bring to a boil and pour over the pork. Cover and cook on the low setting for 6 to 7 hours, or until the pork is tender.

PORK CHOPS in SUMPTUOUS THREE-MUSHROOM SAUCE

This dish features brown, shiitake and portobello mushrooms, taking it quite a step up from the pork chops my mom used to cook in canned mushroom soup. It tastes even more deluxe when steamed asparagus and Whipped Yukon Gold Potatoes (page 200) are served alongside.

preparation time	•	25 minutes
slow cooker time	•	6–7 hours
makes	•	4 servings

ERIC'S OPTIONS
Instead of pork, try veal chops in this recipe. If you like chicken, use four 7 oz (200 g) boneless, skinless chicken breasts in place of the pork. The cooking time remains the same. To simplify things, use only one type of mushroom in this recipe, such as white or brown.

2 Tbsp (30 mL) vegetable oil

Four 7 oz (200 g) pork chops

Salt and freshly ground black pepper to taste

½ lb (250 g) brown mushrooms, sliced (see Buying and Storing White and Brown Mushrooms on page 121)

¼ lb (125 g) fresh shiitake mushrooms, tough stems discarded, caps quartered

One 5-inch (12 cm) wide portobello mushroom, cut into ½-inch (1 cm) cubes

1 medium onion, halved and thinly sliced

¼ cup (60 mL) all-purpose flour

1 garlic clove, minced

3 cups (750 mL) chicken stock

2 tsp (10 mL) dried sage leaves (see Note on page 46)

Place the oil in a skillet set over medium-high heat. Season the chops with salt and pepper. Brown the chops on both sides, then place them in your slow cooker.

Add the mushrooms and onion to the skillet and cook until tender, about 5 minutes. Mix in the flour and garlic and cook for 2 minutes. Slowly mix in the stock. Add the sage, bring the sauce to a simmer, then immediately pour it over the pork. Cover and cook on the low setting for 6 to 7 hours, or until the pork is tender. Plate the chops, top with sauce and serve.

PORK BACK RIBS
in SAUERKRAUT

This German-style meal offers tender pork combined with tangy sauerkraut and a mix of vegetables. Serve these ribs with some boiled potatoes, dill pickles and spicy mustard.

preparation time • **25 minutes**
slow cooker time • **8 hours**
makes • **4 servings**

2 large racks of pork back ribs, each cut into 2-rib pieces

Salt and freshly ground black pepper to taste

1 tsp (5 mL) sweet paprika (see About Paprika on page 71)

28 oz (796 mL) can sauerkraut, rinsed and drained well

1 medium onion, halved and thinly sliced

1 celery stalk, halved lengthwise and sliced

1 large carrot, halved lengthwise and sliced

1 large garlic clove, minced

2 tsp (10 mL) dried sage leaves (see Note on page 46)

2½ cups (625 mL) lager beer or chicken stock

2 Tbsp (30 mL) chopped fresh parsley

ERIC'S OPTIONS
For a sweeter, fruity taste, replace 1 cup (250 mL) of the beer or stock with apple juice.

Position an oven rack 6 inches (15 cm) below the broiler. Set the broiler to high. Place the ribs, meaty side up, on a nonstick baking sheet. Sprinkle with salt, pepper and paprika. Broil the ribs for 3 to 4 minutes, or until richly browned. Turn the ribs over and broil for 2 to 3 minutes more, or until browned on this side. Remove the ribs from the oven.

In your slow cooker, combine the sauerkraut, onion, celery, carrot, garlic and sage. Nestle the ribs into the sauerkraut and pour in the beer or stock. Cover and cook on the low setting for 8 hours, or until the ribs are tender.

Divide the sauerkraut, vegetables and ribs among 4 plates, sprinkle with parsley and serve.

PORK BACK RIBS with BOURBON, CHIPOTLE and MAPLE

These ribs are falling-off-the-bone tender and smoky-tasting thanks to the chipotle pepper, and tastily sauced thanks to the bourbon and maple syrup. I like to serve this with baked potatoes, corn on the cob and Sweet and Tangy Six-Vegetable Coleslaw (page 167).

preparation time	•	15 minutes
slow cooker time	•	8 hours
makes	•	4 servings

Vegetable oil for the grill

2 large racks of pork back ribs, each cut into 2-rib pieces

Salt and freshly ground black pepper to taste

1¾ **cups (435 mL)** barbecue sauce

½ **cup (125 mL)** bourbon

½ **cup (125 mL)** unsweetened apple juice

¼ **cup (60 mL)** maple syrup (see About Maple Syrup on page 108)

¼ **cup (60 mL)** fresh lime juice

1–2 chipotle peppers, finely chopped (see Note on page 61)

ERIC'S OPTIONS

If you don't have an indoor or outdoor grill, enrich the color of the ribs before setting them in your slow cooker by broiling them. See the method for Pork Back Ribs in Sauerkraut (page 105) for how to do this.

Preheat an indoor or outdoor grill to high heat. Lightly oil the bars of the grill.

Season the ribs with salt and pepper. Grill the ribs for 3 to 4 minutes per side, or until nicely charred but not cooked through. Set the ribs in your slow cooker, bone side down. Place the remaining ingredients in a bowl and whisk to combine. Pour this mixture over the ribs. Cover and cook on the low setting for 8 hours, or until the ribs are tender.

ABOUT MAPLE SYRUP

During the summer growing season, maple trees that are tapped for their sap in spring—such as the sugar, red and silver maple tree—accumulate starch. That starch stays in the tree during winter's dormant period. When spring hits and things begin to thaw, enzymes change the starch into sugar, which mixes with the water coming up from the roots, creating a sap with a slightly sweet taste.

The sap, which is over 90 percent water, is heated and greatly reduced until sweet and syrupy. Depending on the concentration of the sap, it can take 2¾ gallons (10 L) of sap to make 1 cup (250 mL) of syrup. That's why maple syrup is more expensive than other syrups on the market.

The concentrated sap contains minerals, organic acids and other tastes that the tree's terroir (soil and surroundings) bring to the table, which gives maple syrup a distinct, somewhat earthy taste. That makes maple syrup a decadent and interesting ingredient to use when you need to impart a uniquely sweet flavor to a wide range of dishes, both savory and sweet.

In Canada, there are three grades of maple syrup: Canada No. 1, 2 and 3. The grades are determined primarily by the syrup's color, which could be extra light, light, medium, amber or dark. The lighter the syrup, the higher the grade and the more delicate the flavor. The darker the syrup, the lower the grade and the more robust the flavor. You can use any grade of maple syrup for recipes in this book, depending on your taste preference.

SWEET-and-SOUR PORK with GINGER and PINEAPPLE

There's no need to brown the meat in this recipe. As the pork slowly simmers it tastily absorbs the flavor and the color of the sweet-and-sour sauce surrounding it. Serve this with steamed rice or Cashew Fried Rice (page 182).

preparation time	•	25 minutes
slow cooker time	•	6–8 hours
makes	•	6 servings

⅓ cup (80 mL) ketchup

¼ cup (60 mL) rice vinegar

3 Tbsp (45 mL) golden brown sugar

1 Tbsp (15 mL) soy sauce

1 Tbsp (15 mL) cornstarch

1 large garlic clove, chopped

1 Tbsp (15 mL) peeled, chopped fresh ginger (see About Fresh Ginger on page 30)

1½ lb (750 g) boneless pork shoulder steak, cut into ½-inch (1 cm) cubes

19 oz (540 mL) can unsweetened pineapple chunks

14 oz (398 mL) can tomato sauce

1 medium green bell pepper, cubed

1 medium onion, halved and sliced

Salt and freshly ground black pepper to taste

2 green onions, thinly sliced

ERIC'S OPTIONS
Make sweet-and-sour chicken by replacing the pork with an equal weight of boneless, skinless chicken thighs or breasts, cut into cubes. Make spicy sweet-and-sour pork by adding 2 tsp (10 mL) hot Asian-style chili sauce to the mix of ingredients used to flavor the pork.

Place the ketchup, vinegar, sugar, soy sauce, cornstarch, garlic and ginger in your slow cooker and whisk to combine. Mix in the pork, pineapple with its juice, tomato sauce, bell pepper and onion. Cover and cook on the low setting for 6 to 8 hours, or until the pork is tender. Season the pork with salt and pepper. Sprinkle servings of the pork with green onion.

PORK CHILI with a MEDLEY of BEANS

It's easy to add an interesting and nutritious mix of legumes to a chili dish if you use cans of bean medley. These include a mix of beans, depending on the maker, but usually involve kidney beans, chickpeas, romano beans and black-eyed peas. They can be found at most supermarkets alongside the other canned beans. Serve this chili with tortilla chips for dunking or with Cornbread with Pepper Jack Cheese (page 159).

1½ lb (750 g) lean ground pork

Two 19 oz (540 mL) cans bean medley, drained and rinsed

28 oz (796 mL) can diced tomatoes

28 oz (796 mL) can crushed tomatoes

1½ cups (375 mL) lager beer or chicken stock

1 medium onion, diced

1 medium green bell pepper, diced

1 cup (250 mL) frozen corn kernels

2 Tbsp (30 mL) golden brown sugar

1 Tbsp (15 mL) chili powder

2 tsp (10 mL) ground cumin

2 tsp (10 mL) oregano

1–2 tsp (5–10 mL) hot pepper sauce

Salt and freshly ground black pepper to taste

3 green onions, thinly sliced

preparation time • 20 minutes
slow cooker time • 8 hours
makes • 8 servings

ERIC'S OPTIONS
Instead of pork, make this with ground beef or turkey. Dress up bowls of this chili by topping them with a dollop of sour cream and some grated Monterey Jack or cheddar cheese.

Place the pork in a pot and set over medium heat. Cook, stirring frequently, until the meat is cooked through and crumbly. Drain the pork well and place it in your slow cooker. Mix in the beans, diced and crushed tomatoes, beer, onion, bell pepper, corn, brown sugar, chili powder, cumin, oregano and hot pepper sauce. Cover and cook on the low setting for 8 hours. Season the chili with salt and pepper. Sprinkle servings with green onion.

ITALIAN SAUSAGE, POTATO and BEAN STEW

This sustaining stew is filled with budget-friendly ingredients, including juicy sausage, filling potato and nutritious beans. Serve this with slices of Rosemary Flatbread (page 161) or Roasted Garlic Bread (page 154).

preparation time	•	30 minutes
slow cooker time	•	6 hours
makes	•	4 servings

3–4 mild, medium or hot Italian sausages

2 cups (500 mL) chicken stock

1 Tbsp (15 mL) all-purpose flour

19 oz (540 mL) can romano or white kidney beans, drained, rinsed in cold water and drained again

14 oz (398 mL) can diced tomatoes

3 medium red-skinned potatoes (unpeeled), cut in ½-inch (1 cm) cubes

1 medium onion, diced

1 medium green bell pepper, diced

1–2 garlic cloves, minced

2 tsp (10 mL) ground cumin

1 tsp (5 mL) chili powder

Salt and freshly ground black pepper to taste

2 green onions, thinly sliced

ERIC'S OPTIONS
Instead of Italian sausages, try another type of fresh sausage in this stew, such as chorizo or turkey sausage. For added color, at the end of cooking, swirl 2 to 3 cups (500 to 750 mL) of fresh baby spinach into the stew. Cover and cook for 3 to 4 minutes more, or just until the spinach is wilted.

Preheat the oven to 425°F (220°C). Place the sausages in a nonstick or parchment paper–lined baking dish. Roast for 20 minutes, turning once, or until cooked through. Let the sausages cool for 10 minutes, then cut them into ½-inch (1 cm) slices.

Place the stock and flour in your slow cooker and whisk until the flour is completely dissolved. Add the sliced sausages, beans, tomatoes, potatoes, onion, bell pepper, garlic, cumin and chili powder and mix to combine. Cover and cook on the low setting for 6 hours, or until the vegetables are tender. Season the stew with salt and pepper. To serve, sprinkle bowls of stew with green onions.

PULLED PORK SANDWICHES

I'm not going to say this pork is as good as if it had been cooked over a wood-fired barbecue pit, but it is slow-cooked, very succulent and dripping with barbecue sauce. Serve the sandwiches with pickles, Sweet and Tangy Six-Vegetable Coleslaw and Crispy Oven Fries (pictured; recipes on page 167 and page 202).

preparation time • 15 minutes
slow cooker time • 8 hours
finishing time • 20 minutes
makes • 8 sandwiches

ERIC'S OPTIONS
Instead of sandwiches, make pulled pork burritos by rolling the meat in tortillas with diced onion, shredded lettuce and grated Monterey Jack cheese.

1½ cups (375 mL) barbecue sauce

1¼ cups (310 mL) lager beer or chicken stock

¼ cup (60 mL) packed golden brown sugar

¼ cup (60 mL) apple cider vinegar

2 tsp (10 mL) sweet paprika (see About Paprika on page 71)

2 tsp (10 mL) chili powder

2 tsp (10 mL) ground cumin

1 tsp (5 mL) salt

3 lb (1.5 kg) boneless pork shoulder roast

2 Tbsp (30 mL) olive oil

8 hamburger buns or large crusty rolls, split and warmed

Place the barbecue sauce, beer, brown sugar and vinegar in your slow cooker and whisk to combine. On a wide plate, mix together the paprika, chili powder, cumin and salt. Set the pork on the plate and roll it to coat evenly with the spice mix.

Place the oil in a large skillet set over medium-high heat. Add the pork and sear on all sides. (See How to Sear Meat Properly on page 119.) Set the pork in the slow cooker, turning it to coat with the sauce. Cover and cook on the low setting for 8 hours, or until very tender. Remove the pork from the sauce and set it in a bowl. Skim off any fat from the surface of the sauce, then cover and keep the sauce warm in the slow cooker.

When the pork is cool enough to handle, shred it with 2 forks. Add the meat to the sauce, cover and heat through for 10 minutes. Pile the pork into the buns and serve.

BEANS with CANADIAN BACON and BLACKSTRAP MOLASSES

I do enjoy a big pot of baked beans. These beans (pictured on page 157) are not actually baked, but they taste like they have been after simmering all day in my slow cooker with flavor-enhancing ingredients. I like to serve these sweet and smoky-tasting beans with tangy Buttermilk Biscuits (page 156).

preparation time • **45 minutes**
slow cooker time • **8 hours**
makes • **6–8 serving**

2 cups (500 mL) dried small white or navy beans

1¼ cups (310 mL) ketchup

1¼ cups (310 mL) barbecue sauce

1 cup (250 mL) chicken stock

1 cup (250 mL) water or beer

⅓ lb (170 g) Canadian (back) bacon, diced

¼ cup (60 mL) blackstrap molasses

¼ cup (60 mL) packed golden brown sugar

1 large onion, diced

1 Tbsp (15 mL) Dijon mustard

ERIC'S OPTIONS
Instead of Canadian bacon, use cubes of smoked turkey or ham. Or make the beans a vegetarian dish by omitting the bacon and using vegetable stock instead of chicken stock.

Place the beans in a large pot and cover with 10 cups (2.5 L) of cold water. Bring to a boil, then reduce the heat until the water is gently simmering. Cook the beans until just tender, about 45 minutes. Drain the beans well. Place all the remaining ingredients in your slow cooker and mix well. Mix in the beans. Cover and cook on the low setting for 8 hours.

ABOUT MOLASSES

For something that is technically considered a by-product, molasses has made a very tasty impression on foods we know and love. Gingerbread, muffins, licorice confections and barbecue sauce are just a handful of the creations enriched by what I call the "black gold" of the culinary world.

When sugar cane and sugar beets are refined to make sugar, the residual syrupy juice is placed in a machine where centrifugal force removes the sugar crystals (the basis of sugar). The liquid that remains is called molasses.

The syrupy juice is boiled three times, giving us three types of molasses. Fancy molasses, also called light molasses because of its lighter color and taste, comes from the first boiling. It has the highest sugar content because only a modest amount of sugar crystals has been removed. It can be used as a sweetener for coffee or a topping for toast, pancakes or waffles—hence its other name, table molasses. Fancy molasses can also be used in recipes that will be cooked, or to add a more subtle and sweeter taste and lighter color to baked goods.

Cooking molasses, also called dark molasses, is produced from the second boiling of the liquid. It is darker, richer and a touch more bitter than fancy molasses. These qualities make it ideal for cooking. It can add a robust flavor to sauces, glazes, cookies, loaves, braised dishes and much more.

Intensely dark blackstrap molasses is the liquid that remains after the third extraction of the sugar crystals. The word blackstrap is derived in part from the Dutch *stroop*, which means syrup. Because more sugar crystals have been extracted at this stage, the molasses has a much more intense aroma, is less sweet and has a bitter bite. Thanks to those qualities, I like to use blackstrap molasses in recipes that will benefit from its sharper taste and the dark and rich color it can impart, such as baked beans.

Fancy and cooking molasses are good sources of vitamin B, iron and calcium. Blackstrap molasses is sometimes sold as a health food because it is less sweet and has higher concentrations of these nutrients.

BEEF, VEAL AND LAMB

BEEF GOULASH

Goulash is Hungary's most famous dish. It is now prepared by cooks around the world who are looking to make something hearty and delicious to eat. Like many dishes that have been prepared for generations, the exact mix and amounts of ingredients that go into making beef goulash can vary from household to household, but most, such as mine, will include onions, tomatoes, green pepper and, of course, paprika. Serve this with egg noodles and, to mop up any leftover sauce, Buttermilk Biscuits (page 156).

preparation time • **30 minutes**
slow cooker time • **6–8 hours**
makes • **8 servings**

ERIC'S OPTIONS
For added richness, top servings of the goulash with a dollop of sour cream.

2 lb (1 kg) top round beef roast, cut into ¾-inch (2 cm) cubes

Salt and freshly ground black pepper to taste

⅓ cup (80 mL) all-purpose flour

¼ cup (60 mL) olive oil

2¾ cups (685 mL) beef stock

2 medium white-skinned potatoes (unpeeled), diced

2 medium carrots, diced

1 large onion, diced

1 large green bell pepper, diced

2–3 garlic cloves, chopped

2 Tbsp (30 mL) sweet paprika (see About Paprika on page 71)

2 Tbsp (30 mL) tomato paste

2 tsp (10 mL) marjoram

1 bay leaf

2 green onions, thinly sliced

Season the beef with salt and pepper and coat it in flour. Place the oil in a large skillet set over medium-high heat. When hot, sear the beef in batches, setting the browned pieces in your slow cooker as you go.

Add the stock, potatoes, carrots, onion, bell pepper, garlic, paprika, tomato paste, marjoram and bay leaf. The mixture will look quite thick, but it will thin as the vegetables cook and liquid seeps from them. Cover and cook on the low setting for 6 to 8 hours, or until the beef is very tender. Add additional salt and pepper if needed. Garnish servings of the goulash with sliced green onion.

HOW TO SEAR MEAT PROPERLY

If you've ever wondered why those pork chops or cubes of stewing beef you were hoping to turn a rich brown seem to steam rather than sear in the skillet, you've likely made a few simple missteps during the process. Prepackaged meats, including pork, beef, veal and chicken, may have small pools of liquid in the package. If you want the meat to sear properly, you need to get rid of any moisture on the meat before cooking. To do so, simply pat the meat dry with a paper towel.

Once that's done, you can still end up with meat that does not properly sear if you add it to the skillet before the latter is properly heated. If you add the meat when the skillet and oil are only slightly warm, there's not much chance of it quickly searing and browning nicely.

Lastly, even if you add the meat to a nice hot skillet, if you add too much at once, it still won't brown properly as the skillet will cool down. Also, any moisture in the meat will not have a chance to evaporate, which will cause the meat to steam, rather than sear.

BEEF BURGUNDY-STYLE

Don't be concerned about how thick this French-style stew appears before the cooking begins. Moisture is released from the meat and vegetables during the hours of slow simmering, turning it into a deliciously saucy dish. Serve this with boiled potatoes, plain or dressed up, such as Boiled Mini Potatoes with Grainy Mustard and Lemon (page 207).

2 cups (500 mL) beef stock

1 cup (250 mL) red wine

⅓ cup (80 mL) all-purpose flour

2 Tbsp (30 mL) Dijon mustard

1½ lb (750 g) cubed stewing beef

4 bacon slices, cut into ¼-inch (6 mm) wide strips, cooked crisply and drained well

¾ lb (375 g) white or brown mushrooms, quartered (see Buying and Storing White and Brown Mushrooms on facing page)

1 medium onion, diced

1 medium carrot, quartered lengthwise and sliced

2 garlic cloves, minced

2 bay leaves

½ tsp (2.5 mL) dried thyme

Salt and freshly ground black pepper to taste

2 Tbsp (30 mL) chopped fresh parsley

preparation time	•	20 minutes
slow cooker time	•	6–8 hours
makes	•	6 servings

ERIC'S OPTIONS
Instead of regular onions, add 24 to 30 pearl onions, fresh (peeled) or frozen, to the stew at the start of cooking.

Place the stock, wine, flour and mustard in your slow cooker and whisk until the flour is completely dissolved. Mix in the beef, bacon, mushrooms, onion, carrot, garlic, bay leaves and thyme. Cover and cook on the low setting for 6 to 8 hours, or until the beef is tender. Season with salt and pepper. Sprinkle with chopped parsley to serve.

BUYING AND STORING WHITE AND BROWN MUSHROOMS

White (also called button) and brown (also called crimini) mushrooms are the two most common mushrooms you see for sale in supermarkets. They can be used interchangeably in recipes, but brown mushrooms offer a richer and more earthy flavor and have a firmer texture than mild-tasting white mushrooms.

When buying either type of mushroom, look for firm, unblemished ones that are evenly colored. The area where the cap attaches to the stem should be tightly closed; if the gills of the mushroom are very visible, the mushroom is past its prime.

To store, keep the mushrooms refrigerated in the paper bag in which you bought them. They're best used as soon as possible, but they will keep for several days if they were in very fine condition when you bought them.

If you like to wash mushrooms before using them, gently wipe them clean with a damp paper towel. You could also fill a bowl with cold water, add the mushrooms and very quickly and gently rinse them. Don't let them soak in the water or they'll start to absorb it. Lift the mushrooms out of the water and dry on paper towels.

BEEF DAUBE

The beef in this dark, rich, French-style dish is given a wonderful flavor even before it makes it into the slow cooker. After slices of garlic are cooked until golden in a skillet and removed, the beef is seared in the remaining oil and infused with a divine, garlicky taste. For an ultradecadent meal, serve this with Roquefort and Chive Mashed Potatoes (pictured; recipe page 198).

¼ cup (60 mL) olive oil

4 large garlic cloves, halved and thinly sliced

2 lb (1 kg) boneless chuck or blade steak, cut into
    1½-inch (4 cm) cubes

Salt and freshly ground black pepper to taste

3 medium carrots, halved lengthwise and sliced

1 large onion, diced

3 Tbsp (45 mL) all-purpose flour

1 cup (250 mL) beef stock

1 cup (250 mL) red wine

14 oz (398 mL) can diced tomatoes

2 Tbsp (30 mL) tomato paste

2 bay leaves

½ tsp (2.5 mL) dried thyme

Pinch ground cloves

Chopped fresh parsley to taste

Continued . . .

preparation time	•	30 minutes
slow cooker time	•	6–8 hours
makes	•	4–6 serving

ERIC'S OPTIONS
Make lamb daube by replacing the beef with a 2 lb (1 kg) piece of boneless lamb leg, cubed.

BEEF DAUBE
(*continued*)

Place the olive oil in a large skillet set over medium-low to medium heat. Add the garlic and cook until lightly golden and aromatic, 4 to 5 minutes. Remove the skillet from the heat. Lift the garlic out of the skillet with a slotted spoon and set it in your slow cooker.

Return the skillet to the stovetop and increase heat to medium-high. Season the beef with salt and pepper, then sear in batches, setting the browned pieces in your slow cooker as you go. (See How to Sear Meat Properly on page 119.)

Add the carrot and onion to the skillet and cook for 3 to 4 minutes. Stir in the flour and cook for 2 minutes more. Slowly, while stirring, mix in the stock. Mix in the wine, diced tomatoes, tomato paste, bay leaves, thyme and cloves and bring to a simmer. Pour this mixture over the beef and stir to combine. Cover and cook on the low setting for 6 to 8 hours, or until the beef is very tender. Sprinkle servings with chopped parsley.

COUNTRY-STYLE BEEF and VEGETABLE STEW

I call this country-style stew because it's not a lot of fuss to make. Basically you throw everything into your slow cooker, turn it on and get on with doing more important things, such as having coffee with your neighbor down the road. I like to serve this with Whipped Yukon Gold Potatoes (page 200).

preparation time	•	20 minutes
slow cooker time	•	6–8 hours
finishing time	•	10 minutes
makes	•	4 servings

ERIC'S OPTIONS
Make lamb and vegetable stew by replacing the beef with cubes of lamb stew meat. Instead of thyme, try another herb such as rosemary.

2¾ cups (685 mL) beef stock

¼ cup (60 mL) all-purpose flour

3 Tbsp (45 mL) tomato paste

1¼ lb (625 g) cubed stewing beef

2 medium celery stalks, halved lengthwise and sliced

2 garlic cloves, minced

1 medium onion, diced

1 medium carrot, halved lengthwise and sliced

1 medium parsnip, halved lengthwise and sliced

1 tsp (5 mL) dried thyme

⅓ cup (80 mL) frozen corn kernels

⅓ cup (80 mL) frozen peas

Salt and freshly ground black pepper to taste

2 Tbsp (30 mL) chopped fresh parsley

Place the stock, flour and tomato paste in your slow cooker and whisk until the flour is completely dissolved. Mix in the beef, celery, garlic, onion, carrot, parsnip and thyme. Cover and cook on the low setting for 6 to 8 hours, or until the beef is tender. Swirl in the corn and peas, cover and cook for 10 minutes more, or until the corn and peas are heated through. Season the stew with salt and pepper. Sprinkle servings of the stew with chopped fresh parsley.

SAUERKRAUT-STUFFED BEEF ROULADEN

Rouladen is a German-style dish where very thinly sliced pieces of beef, often cut from the round, are rolled around a filling, in this recipe sauerkraut. You can buy the meat for rouladen cut and ready to use at most supermarkets, or ask the butcher at your local butcher shop to cut it for you. I like to serve this version of rouladen with Mixed Vegetable Rice Pilaf (page 184) or Garlic Mashed Yukon Gold Potatoes with Kale (page 194).

preparation time • 35 minutes
slow cooker time • 7–8 hours
makes • 4 servings

ERIC'S OPTIONS
Instead of rolling a carrot and celery stick inside each rouladen, roll a long, thin slice of dill pickle. Instead of regular Dijon mustard, try using whole grain Dijon, which has a coarser texture.

8 very thin pieces beef rouladen (each about 8 inches/20 cm long and 4 inches/10 cm wide)

8 tsp (40 mL) Dijon mustard

Eight 3- to 4-inch (8 to 10 cm) carrot sticks

Eight 3- to 4-inch (8 to 10 cm) celery sticks

2 cups (500 mL) sauerkraut, rinsed and drained well

Salt and freshly ground black pepper to taste

3 Tbsp (45 mL) vegetable oil

2½ cups (625 mL) beef stock

¼ cup (60 mL) all-purpose flour

Set a piece of rouladen flat on a work surface. Brush the top of it with 1 tsp (5 mL) of the mustard. Set a carrot and celery stick at one end of the meat and top with ¼ cup (60 mL) of sauerkraut. Roll the meat into a cylinder and secure with string or a toothpick. Repeat with the remaining rouladen and fillings. Season rouladen with salt and pepper.

Continued . . .

SAUERKRAUT-STUFFED BEEF ROULADEN
(*continued*)

Place the oil in a large skillet set over medium-high heat. When hot, add the stuffed rouladen, in batches if necessary, and brown on all sides. Set the rouladen in your slow cooker.

Drain the excess oil from the skillet. Place the stock and flour in a bowl and whisk to combine. Pour this mixture into the skillet. Bring to a boil and cook until slightly thickened, about 2 minutes. Pour this mixture over the rouladen. Cover and cook on the low setting for 7 to 8 hours, or until the beef is very tender.

To serve, remove the string or toothpicks from the rouladen. Set 2 pieces of rouladen on each of 4 plates. Top with some of the sauce in the slow cooker and serve.

OYSTER MUSHROOM–STUFFED BEEF ROULADEN

Oyster mushrooms were given that name because of their oyster-like shape and creamy white to grey color. They have a mild flavor and a delicate, silky texture. When sliced into strips and sautéed they make a fine filling for these rouladen. Serve this with egg noodles or boiled potatoes and Candied Carrots and Parsnips with Peas (page 213).

preparation time • 35 minutes
slow cooker time • 7–8 hours
makes • 4 servings

ERIC'S OPTIONS
If you like cooking with wine, replace ½ to 1 cup (125 to 250 mL) of the beef stock in this recipe with an equal amount of red wine.

¾ lb (375 g) oyster mushrooms

4 Tbsp (60 mL) vegetable oil, divided

2 garlic cloves, minced

Salt and freshly ground black pepper to taste

8 pieces beef rouladen (each about 8 inches/20 cm long and 4 inches/10 cm wide) (see recipe introduction on page 127)

2½ cups (625 mL) beef stock

¼ cup (60 mL) all-purpose flour

2 Tbsp (30 mL) whole grain Dijon mustard

½ tsp (2.5 mL) dried tarragon

2 green onions, thinly sliced

Separate the clusters of oyster mushrooms into individual mushrooms. Trim off and discard the tough lower stems. Cut the mushrooms into thin, lengthwise strips. Pour 1 Tbsp (15 mL) of the oil into a large skillet set over medium-high heat. When hot, add the mushrooms, garlic and salt and pepper and cook until the mushrooms are tender, about 3 minutes. Transfer the mushrooms to a bowl and cool to room temperature. Clean the skillet.

Continued . . .

OYSTER MUSHROOM-STUFFED BEEF ROULADEN (*continued*)

Set a piece of rouladen flat on a work surface. Place one-eighth of the mushrooms in a row at one end of the meat. Roll the meat into a cylinder and secure with string or a toothpick. Repeat with the remaining rouladen and mushrooms. Season rouladen with salt and pepper.

Place the remaining 3 Tbsp (45 mL) oil in the skillet and set over medium-high heat. When hot, add the stuffed rouladen, in batches if necessary, and brown on all sides. Set the rouladen in your slow cooker. Drain the excess oil from the skillet. Place the stock, flour, Dijon mustard and tarragon in a bowl and whisk to combine. Pour this mixture into the skillet. Bring to a boil and cook until slightly thickened, about 2 minutes. Pour this mixture over the rouladen. Cover and cook on the low setting for 7 to 8 hours, or until the beef is tender.

To serve, remove the string or toothpicks from the rouladen. Set 2 pieces of rouladen on each of 4 plates. Top with some of the sauce from the slow cooker and sprinkle with green onion to serve.

BEEF SHORT RIBS SMOTHERED in ONIONS and BARBECUE SAUCE

Cooking the short ribs in a very hot oven for 30 minutes before setting them in your slow cooker browns them deeply and renders out quite a bit of the internal fat that this cut can contain. To make a fine meal, serve them with some steamed and buttered green beans and Roasted Potatoes with Honey, Dijon and Pepper (page 203).

preparation time • 35 minutes
slow cooker time • 6–8 hours
finishing time • 1–2 minutes
makes • 4 servings

ERIC'S OPTIONS
You can adjust the taste of these ribs to your liking by simply replacing the more neutral regular barbecue sauce with your preferred variety—hot and spicy, or sweet and smoky, for example.

8 meaty beef short ribs

Salt and freshly ground black pepper to taste

2 medium onions, halved and thinly sliced

1¾ cups (435 mL) barbecue sauce

¾ cup (185 mL) beef stock

¾ cup (185 mL) beer or water

2 Tbsp (30 mL) cider vinegar

2 Tbsp (30 mL) golden brown sugar

1 Tbsp (15 mL) chopped fresh rosemary

2 green onions, thinly sliced

Preheat the oven to 450°F (230°C).

Set the ribs in a single layer, bone side down, in a roasting pan and season with salt and pepper. Roast the ribs for 30 minutes, or until richly browned, then drain off any excess fat.

Spread half the onions in the bottom of your slow cooker. Set the ribs on top of the onions, bone side down. Combine the remaining ingredients, except the green onion, in a bowl and pour over the short ribs. Cover and cook on the low setting for 6 to 8 hours, or until the ribs are very tender.

To serve, set 2 ribs on each of 4 plates. Skim off any fat from the sauce, then taste and add salt and pepper, if needed. Top the ribs with some sauce and sprinkle with green onion to serve.

HOISIN CHILI BEEF BACK RIBS

Relatively inexpensive beef back ribs are the bones left behind after a butcher removes the rib eye from a prime rib. In between those bones is a generous amount of succulent meat that can taste heavenly when slowly cooked until tender. In this recipe (pictured on page 215), that is done Asian-style, with ingredients such as spicy chili and hoisin sauce. Serve this with Asian-style egg noodles or steamed rice and Mixed Vegetable Stir-Fry in Sweet Chili Sauce (page 214).

8 meaty beef back ribs, trimmed of visible excess fat

Salt and freshly ground black pepper to taste

1 cup (250 mL) water

1 cup (250 mL) beef stock

¾ cup (185 mL) hoisin sauce

½ cup (125 mL) Chinese rice wine or dry sherry

⅓ cup (80 mL) soy sauce

2 tsp (10 mL) hot Asian-style chili sauce, or to taste

2 garlic cloves, minced

1 Tbsp (15 mL) cornstarch

2 green onions, thinly sliced

preparation time	• 35 minutes
slow cooker time	• 8 hours
finishing time	• 1–2 minutes
makes	• 4 servings

ERIC'S OPTIONS

Give the ribs added texture by sprinkling them with some toasted sesame seeds after plating them and topping them with the sauce.

Preheat the oven to 450°F (230°C).

Set the ribs in a single layer, bone side down, in a roasting pan and season with salt and pepper. Roast the ribs for 30 minutes, or until richly browned, then drain away any excess fat. Set the ribs in your slow cooker, bone side down.

Place the water, stock, hoisin sauce, rice wine, soy sauce, chili sauce, garlic and cornstarch in a medium bowl and whisk to combine. Pour this mixture over the ribs. Cover and cook the ribs on the low setting for 8 hours, or until the ribs are very tender.

To serve, set 2 ribs on each of 4 plates. Skim off any fat from the sauce, then taste and add salt and pepper, if needed. Top the ribs with some of the sauce, sprinkle with green onions and serve.

ABOUT HOISIN SAUCE

Hoisin sauce, sold in jars at most supermarkets and Asian food stores, is a thick sauce widely used in Chinese cooking. North American cooks seeking to infuse an Asian-style taste into a dish they are preparing also use it. Its color can range from reddish-brown to almost black, depending on the maker. This intensely flavored sauce is made by blending cooked soybeans with flavorings such as various spices, garlic, sugar and vinegar. Hoisin sauce is often used as a condiment or as a flavoring ingredient for a wide range of meat, poultry, seafood and vegetarian dishes. Once opened, it can be stored in the refrigerator for several months.

SAKE SOY BRAISED BEEF SHORT RIBS

Sake is a Japanese-style wine made from fermented rice. It's not only lovely to sip, but also to cook with. I like to serve these tender ribs with steamed baby bok choy and Ginger Mashed Squash (pictured; recipe page 209).

8 thick and meaty beef short ribs

Salt and freshly ground black pepper to taste

1 medium onion, halved and thinly sliced

One 2-inch (5 cm) piece of fresh ginger, peeled, halved lengthwise and thinly sliced (see About Fresh Ginger on page 30)

3 garlic cloves, halved lengthwise and thinly sliced

½ **cup (125 mL)** soy sauce

½ **cup (125 mL)** sake

½ **cup (125 mL)** beef stock

½ **cup (125 mL)** water

¼ **cup (60 mL)** packed golden brown sugar

2 Tbsp (30 mL) cornstarch

2 green onions, thinly sliced

preparation time	• 35 minutes
slow cooker time	• 6–8 hours
finishing time	• 1–2 minutes
makes	• 4 servings

ERIC'S OPTIONS
For spicy sake soy short ribs, add 2 tsp (10 mL) of hot Asian-style chili sauce to the liquid ingredients you pour over the ribs.

Preheat oven to 450°F (230°C). Set the ribs in a single layer, bone side down, in a roasting pan. Season them with salt and pepper. Roast the ribs for 30 minutes, or until richly browned, then drain off any excess fat.

Spread half the onion, half the ginger and half the garlic in your slow cooker. Set the ribs into the slow cooker, bone side down. Place the soy sauce, sake, beef stock, water, brown sugar and cornstarch in a bowl and whisk to combine. Pour this over the ribs, then sprinkle them with the remaining onion, ginger and garlic. Cover and cook on the low setting for 6 to 8 hours, or until the ribs are very tender.

To serve, set 2 ribs on each of 4 plates. Skim off any fat from the sauce, then taste and add salt and pepper, if needed. Top the ribs with some sauce and sprinkle with green onion to serve.

SHREDDED BEEF SANDWICHES

The meat in this dish is slow-cooked, then pulled into tasty shreds, a technique similar to that used in Pulled Pork Sandwiches (page 113). Of course, beef becomes ridiculously succulent after slow-cooking in barbecue sauce, onions, garlic and other good things. Serve these sandwiches with dill pickles, corn on the cob and New Red and White Potato Salad (page 172).

1½ cups (375 mL) barbecue sauce

1½ cups (375 mL) beef stock

2 medium onions, halved and thinly sliced

2 garlic cloves, minced

2 Tbsp (30 mL) Dijon mustard

2 Tbsp (30 mL) balsamic vinegar

2 Tbsp (30 mL) golden brown sugar

2 Tbsp (30 mL) vegetable oil

3 lb (1.5 kg) top round beef roast

Salt and freshly ground black pepper to taste

6–8 burger buns or large crusty rolls

preparation time • 10 minutes
slow cooker time • 8 hours
finishing time • 15 minutes
makes • 6–8 servings

ERIC'S OPTIONS
If you don't have any beef stock, but you do have lager beer, use it in the same volume in this recipe instead.

Place the barbecue sauce, stock, onions, garlic, mustard, vinegar and brown sugar in your slow cooker and mix to combine. Place the oil in a large skillet set over medium-high heat. Season the beef with salt and pepper and sear on all sides (see How to Sear Meat Properly on page 119). Set the beef in your slow cooker and turn it to coat with the sauce. Cover and cook on the low setting for 8 hours, or until the beef is very tender.

Lift the beef out of the slow cooker and set it in a large bowl. Taste the sauce and season with salt and pepper, if needed. Keep the sauce warm in your slow cooker. Let the beef cool for a few minutes, then use 2 forks to pull it into shreds. Stir the shreds of beef back into the sauce. Cover and let the beef heat in the sauce for 10 minutes. Meanwhile, slice the buns in half and warm them up. Pile the meat into the buns and enjoy.

VEAL MEATBALLS in TOMATO SAUCE with FRESH BASIL

The milk helps to give these meatballs (pictured on page 190) a more delicate texture, and the basil adds a lively, fresh flavor and wonderful green color. Serve the meatballs on plain cooked pasta, or on a flavored one such as Spaghetti with Lemon, Chilies and Garlic (page 191).

preparation time • 30 minutes
slow cooker time • 6–8 hours
makes • 4–6 servings

ERIC'S OPTIONS
Make open-faced meatball sandwiches by piling these meatballs onto thick slices of Italian bread. For deluxe meatball sandwiches, scoop the meatballs onto Roasted Garlic Bread (page 154). Make beef meatballs by replacing the veal with ground beef.

1¼ lb (625 g) ground veal

⅓ cup (80 mL) dried breadcrumbs

2 Tbsp (30 mL) milk

1 large egg, beaten

1–2 garlic cloves, minced

1 tsp (5 mL) salt, plus some to taste

½ tsp (2.5 mL) freshly ground black pepper, plus some to taste

28 oz (796 mL) can diced tomatoes

14 oz (398 mL) can crushed tomatoes

½ cup (125 mL) red wine or beef stock

½ tsp (2.5 mL) sugar

Pinch crushed chili flakes

¼ cup (60 mL) chopped fresh basil

Preheat the oven to 375°F (190°C). Line a baking sheet with parchment paper. Place the veal, breadcrumbs, milk, egg, garlic, salt and pepper in a bowl and mix to combine. Moisten your hands with cold water. Roll the meat mixture into 1½-inch (4 cm) balls and set on the prepared baking sheet. Roast for 20 minutes, or until cooked through.

Place the diced tomatoes, crushed tomatoes, wine or stock, sugar and chili flakes in your slow cooker and stir to combine. Drain off any fat from the meatballs and add them to the sauce. Cover and cook on the low setting for 6 to 8 hours, or until the meatballs are tender. Gently stir the fresh basil into the meatballs and serve.

OSSO BUCCO with GREMOLATA

This succulent, slow-cooked veal shank is sprinkled with gremolata, a palate-awakening parsley, citrus zest and garlic mixture. I like to serve this with something that will blend tastily with the sauce, such as creamy polenta or Saffron Risotto (page 188).

Four 7–8 oz (200–250 g) veal shanks

Salt and freshly ground black pepper to taste

¼ cup (60 mL) all-purpose flour

3 Tbsp (45 mL) olive oil

1 small onion, finely diced

1 large celery stalk, finely diced

1 small carrot, finely diced

2–3 garlic cloves, minced

2 tsp (10 mL) dried sage leaves (see Note on page 46)

28 oz (796 mL) can diced tomatoes

½ cup (125 mL) dry white wine

2 Tbsp (30 mL) tomato paste

1 bay leaf

6 sprigs Italian parsley

1 garlic clove, thickly sliced

1 tsp (5 mL) grated lemon zest

1 tsp (5 mL) grated orange zest

preparation time	•	30 minutes
slow cooker time	•	7–8 hours
finishing time	•	1–2 minutes
makes	•	4 servings

ERIC'S OPTIONS
Make lamb osso bucco by replacing the veal shanks with lamb shanks.

Season the veal with salt and pepper, then coat in the flour, shaking off any excess. Place the oil in a large skillet and set over medium-high heat. When hot, add the veal and brown deeply on both sides. Set the veal in your slow cooker.

Add the onion, celery and carrot to the skillet and cook for 2 to 3 minutes. Add the garlic and sage and cook for 1 minute more. Add the diced tomatoes, wine, tomato paste and bay leaf, bring to a simmer and pour over the veal. Cover and cook the veal on the low setting for 7 to 8 hours, or until very tender.

For the gremolata, finely chop the parsley, sliced garlic clove, lemon zest and orange zest together.

To serve, carefully lift the veal shanks out of the slow cooker and set 1 on each of 4 plates. Skim off any fat from the sauce, then taste and add salt and pepper, if needed. Top the veal with some of the sauce and sprinkle with gremolata to serve.

SOUTHERN-STYLE BRAISED VEAL SHANKS

I call this southern-style because the tomatoey braising sauce contains chili powder and cumin, ingredients frequently used in Tex-Mex–style dishes. Serve this with Spanish-Style Brown Rice, and Green Beans with Pecans, Lime and Honey (both pictured; recipes on page 186 and page 212).

preparation time	•	25 minutes
slow cooker time	•	7–8 hours
finishing time	•	1–2 minutes
makes	•	4 servings

ERIC'S OPTIONS
Make southern-style braised lamb shanks by replacing the veal shanks with lamb shanks. Give the shanks a smoky and spicy taste by adding 1 or 2 finely chopped chipotle peppers to the tomato mixture before pouring it over the shanks.

2 tsp (10 mL) ground cumin

2 tsp (10 mL) chili powder

1 tsp (5 mL) dried sage leaves (see Note on page 46)

1 tsp (5 mL) dried oregano

½ tsp (2.5 mL) salt

½ tsp (2.5 mL) freshly ground black pepper

¼ tsp (1 mL) cayenne pepper

Four 7–8 oz (200–250 g) veal shanks

3 Tbsp (45 mL) olive oil

14 oz (398 mL) can tomato sauce

1 cup (250 mL) beef stock

1 medium onion, diced

2 garlic cloves, halved and thinly sliced

1 Tbsp (15 mL) golden brown sugar

2 Tbsp (30 mL) chopped fresh cilantro or sliced green onion (optional)

Combine the cumin, chili powder, sage, oregano, salt, black pepper and cayenne pepper on a wide plate. Place the veal shanks on the plate and turn to coat with the mixture, pressing it on to help it adhere.

Continued . . .

SOUTHERN-STYLE BRAISED VEAL SHANKS
(*continued*)

Place the oil in a large skillet and set over medium-high heat. When hot, add the veal and brown deeply on both sides. Set the veal in your slow cooker.

Combine the tomato sauce, stock, onion, garlic and brown sugar in a bowl, then pour over the shanks. Cover and cook on the low setting for 7 to 8 hours, or until the veal is tender.

To serve, carefully lift the veal shanks out of the slow cooker and set 1 on each of 4 plates. Skim off any fat from the sauce, then taste and add salt and pepper, if needed. Top the veal with some of the sauce and, if desired, sprinkle with cilantro or green onion to serve.

ABOUT LAMB AND VEAL SHANKS

Lamb and veal shanks are cut from the bottom, shin portion of their respective animals' legs. Lamb shanks are sold whole and one of them is just the right size for a single portion.

Veal shanks are quite a bit larger than lamb shanks and so they are usually cut through the bone into single-serving-thick slices.

Both lamb and veal shanks are very tough cuts, but that changes when the meat is slowly braised for several hours. Braising means slowly cooking food with a flavored liquid in a covered cooking vessel. A slow cooker does that job magnificently. As the shanks braise, steam rises from the liquid and slowly and deliciously tenderizes them.

VEAL STROGANOFF

Stroganoff is a famous dish; according to folk wisdom, it may have been named after Count Paul Stroganov, a Russian diplomat and bon vivant who lived in St. Petersburg from 1774 to 1817. Serve this with Broccoli with Lemon Zest, Ginger and Red Pepper (page 210) and Saffron Rice with Parsley (page 185).

preparation time • 25 minutes
slow cooker time • 6 hours
finishing time • 5 minutes
makes • 4 servings

2 cups (500 mL) beef stock

3 Tbsp (45 mL) all-purpose flour

2 Tbsp (30 mL) Dijon mustard

1 Tbsp (15 mL) Worcestershire sauce

½ tsp (2.5 mL) dried thyme

¼ tsp (1 mL) sweet paprika (see About Paprika on page 71)

1¼ lb (625 g) veal cutlets, thinly sliced

Salt and freshly ground black pepper to taste

2 Tbsp (30 mL) olive oil

½ lb (250 g) white mushrooms, sliced (see Buying and Storing White and Brown Mushrooms on page 121)

1 medium onion, halved and thinly sliced

1–2 garlic cloves, minced

½ cup (125 mL) regular or low-fat sour cream

Chopped fresh parsley to taste

ERIC'S OPTIONS
Turn this into beef stroganoff by replacing the veal with an equal amount of sliced beef round steak. Or make chicken stroganoff by replacing the veal with an equal weight of boneless, skinless chicken breast, sliced.

Place the stock, flour, mustard, Worcestershire sauce, thyme and paprika in your slow cooker and whisk until combined. Season the veal with salt and pepper. Heat the oil in a large skillet set over medium-high heat. When hot, brown the veal in batches, setting the cooked pieces in your slow cooker as you go. Mix in the mushrooms, onion and garlic. Cover and cook on the low setting for 6 hours, or until the veal is tender. Stir in the sour cream and heat through for 5 minutes. Season the stroganoff with salt and pepper. Sprinkle servings with chopped parsley.

LAMB STEW with LEEKS and GUINNESS

I came up with this stew when I was looking for a suitable dish to serve for a St. Patrick's Day dinner. Choosing it wasn't rocket science: Ireland is well known for its lamb stew and, of course, its dark and delicious Guinness. Make a very filling meal of this stew by serving it with Garlic Mashed Yukon Gold Potatoes with Kale (page 194) and Soda Bread with Aged Cheddar, Oats and Green Onions (page 152).

1¼ lb (625 g) cubed stewing lamb

Salt and freshly ground black pepper to taste

⅓ cup (80 mL) all-purpose flour

3 Tbsp (45 mL) vegetable oil

2 medium carrots, halved lengthwise and sliced

2 celery stalks, halved lengthwise and sliced

1 large leek, pale green and white part only, halved lengthwise, washed well and sliced (see About Leeks on page 197)

1 garlic clove, minced

1¼ cups (310 mL) beef stock

1½ cups (375 mL) Guinness

1 bay leaf

½ tsp (2.5 mL) dried thyme

½ cup (125 mL) frozen peas

1 Tbsp (15 mL) chopped fresh parsley

preparation time	• 25 minutes
slow cooker time	• 6–8 hours
finishing time	• 5 minutes
makes	• 4 servings

ERIC'S OPTIONS
Make beef, leek and Guinness stew by replacing the lamb with cubes of stewing beef.

Season the lamb with salt and pepper and dredge in the flour, shaking off any excess. Reserve 2 Tbsp (30 mL) of the leftover flour. Heat the oil in a large skillet set over medium-high heat. Cook the lamb in batches until nicely browned, setting the cooked pieces in your slow cooker as you go.

Add the carrots, celery, leek and garlic to the skillet and cook for 3 to 4 minutes. Sprinkle in the reserved flour and mix well to combine. While stirring, slowly pour in the stock and then the Guinness. Add the bay leaf and thyme and bring to a simmer. Pour this mixture over the lamb and stir to combine. Cover and cook on the low setting for 6 to 8 hours, or until the lamb is tender. Mix in the peas, cover and heat them through, about 5 minutes. Taste the stew and add salt and pepper, if needed. Sprinkle servings with chopped fresh parsley.

LAMB CURRY with POTATOES and PEAS

Serve this coconut milk–based, tomatoey lamb curry with steamed basmati rice, Fresh Mint Chutney (page 173) and pappadums. Pappadums, which are great for dunking into the curry, are a wafer-thin, Indian-style flatbread sold at Indian food stores and most supermarkets. Simple cooking instructions are on the box.

3 Tbsp (45 mL) vegetable oil

1½ lb (750 g) cubed stewing lamb

Salt and freshly ground black pepper to taste

1 medium onion, diced

2 Tbsp (30 mL) all-purpose flour

1 Tbsp (15 mL) mild, medium or hot curry powder

½ tsp (2.5 mL) sweet paprika (see About Paprika on page 71)

14 oz (398 mL) can regular or light coconut milk

28 oz (796 mL) can diced tomatoes

2 medium white-skinned potatoes (unpeeled), cubed

2 Tbsp (30 mL) golden brown sugar

1 cup (250 mL) frozen peas

2 Tbsp (30 mL) chopped fresh cilantro or mint

preparation time	• 20 minutes
slow cooker time	• 6–8 hours
finishing time	• 5 minutes
makes	• 6 servings

ERIC'S OPTIONS
Make chicken curry with potatoes and peas by replacing the lamb with an equal weight of boneless, skinless chicken thigh, cubed. The chicken won't take as long to cook, so reduce the cooking time to 5 to 6 hours.

Place the oil in a large skillet set over medium-high heat. Season the lamb with salt and pepper. Brown the lamb in batches, setting the cooked pieces in your slow cooker as you go. Add the onion to the skillet and cook for 2 to 3 minutes. Mix in the flour, curry powder and paprika and cook for 1 minute more. Slowly, while stirring, mix in the coconut milk. Add the diced tomatoes, potatoes and brown sugar, bring to a simmer and pour over the lamb. Cover and cook on the low setting for 6 to 8 hours, or until the lamb is tender.

Mix in the peas and cilantro or mint. Cover and cook for 5 minutes more, or until the peas are heated through.

BRAISED LAMB SHANKS
with 20 CLOVES of GARLIC

Twenty cloves of garlic sounds like a lot, but their flavor mellows deliciously as the lamb slowly cooks. This is an easy-to-make but elegant dish that will impress anyone who loves lamb shanks. Serve it with Brussels Sprouts with Apples and Walnuts (page 216) and Whipped Yukon Gold Potatoes (page 200).

preparation time	•	20 minutes
slow cooker time	•	7–8 hours
finishing time	•	5 minutes
makes	•	4 servings

2 Tbsp (30 mL) olive oil

4 lamb shanks

Salt and freshly ground black pepper to taste

28 oz (796 mL) can diced tomatoes

½ cup (125 mL) red wine or beef stock

1 medium onion, halved and thinly sliced

20 small garlic cloves, kept whole and peeled

2 Tbsp (30 mL) tomato paste

2 Tbsp (30 mL) golden brown sugar

2 tsp (10 mL) chopped fresh rosemary, plus some sprigs for garnish

ERIC'S OPTIONS
Instead of lamb shanks, try using 4 veal shanks.

Place the oil in a large skillet set over medium-high heat. Season the lamb with salt and pepper. When the oil is hot, brown the lamb well on all sides, then set the shanks in your slow cooker. Combine the diced tomatoes, wine or stock, onion, garlic, tomato paste, brown sugar and chopped rosemary in a bowl and pour the mixture over the lamb. Cover and cook on the low setting for 7 to 8 hours, or until the lamb is very tender.

To serve, carefully lift the lamb shanks out of the slow cooker and set 1 on each of 4 plates. Skim off any fat from the sauce, then taste and add salt and pepper, if needed. Top the lamb with some of the sauce, garnish with rosemary sprigs and serve.

LAMB SHANKS BRAISED
with WINE, CITRUS and SPICE

Citrus zest and juice and a flavorful mix of spices in the braising liquid make this a delicious and aromatic way to cook lamb shanks until mouthwateringly tender. Serve them with sautéed or grilled rounds of zucchini and Orzo with Basil and Parmesan Cheese (page 192).

preparation time • 20 minutes
slow cooker time • 7–8 hours
finishing time • 1–2 minutes
makes • 4 servings

2 Tbsp (30 mL) olive oil

4 lamb shanks

Salt and freshly ground black pepper to taste

14 oz (398 mL) can tomato sauce

½ cup (125 mL) red wine

¼ cup (60 mL) fresh orange juice

1 medium onion, halved and thinly sliced

2 garlic cloves, minced

2 Tbsp (30 mL) all-purpose flour

2 Tbsp (30 mL) golden brown sugar

2 Tbsp (30 mL) fresh lemon juice

2 tsp (10 mL) chopped fresh rosemary, plus some sprigs for garnish

1 tsp (5 mL) finely grated orange zest

1 tsp (5 mL) finely grated lemon zest

1 tsp (5 mL) ground cinnamon

1 tsp (5 mL) ground cumin

¼ tsp (1 mL) ground cloves

ERIC'S OPTIONS
Add some spicy heat to the sauce by mixing crushed chili flakes, to taste, into the tomato sauce mixture you pour over the lamb. Instead of lamb shanks, use 4 veal shanks in this recipe.

Place the oil in a large skillet set over medium-high heat. Season the lamb with salt and pepper. When the oil is hot, brown the lamb well on all sides, then set the shanks in your slow cooker. Combine the remaining ingredients in a bowl and pour the mixture over the lamb. Cover and cook on the low setting for 7 to 8 hours, or until tender.

To serve, carefully lift the lamb shanks out of the slow cooker and set 1 on each of 4 plates. Skim off any fat from the sauce, then taste and add salt and pepper, if needed. Top the lamb with some of the sauce, garnish with rosemary sprigs and serve.

DELICIOUS
SIDES

BREADS AND BISCUITS

SODA BREAD with AGED CHEDDAR, OATS and GREEN ONIONS

This delicious loaf is flecked with fiber-rich oats, tangy cheese and fresh-tasting green onion. Use it for sandwiches or serve it alongside any of the soups and stews in this book.

1¼ cups (310 mL) all-purpose flour

1¼ cups (310 mL) whole wheat flour

½ cup (125 mL) large-flake oats

1½ tsp (7.5 mL) baking soda

½ tsp (2.5 mL) salt

¼ cup (60 mL) cold butter, cut into small cubes

1½ cups (310 mL) grated aged cheddar cheese

2 green onions, thinly sliced

1⅓ cups (325 mL) buttermilk

preparation time • 15 minutes
baking time • 30 minutes
makes • 1 loaf

ERIC'S OPTIONS
Instead of cheddar, use another type of tangy cheese in this recipe, such as Gouda or Jarlsberg. Instead of green onion, give the loaf an herbaceous taste by mixing in 2 to 3 tsp (10 to 15 mL) of chopped fresh rosemary.

Preheat the oven to 425°F (220°C). Line a baking sheet with parchment paper.

Place the flours, oats, baking soda and salt in a bowl and whisk well to combine. With your fingers, 2 forks or a pastry cutter, work the butter into the flour mixture until thoroughly distributed. Mix in the cheese and green onions. Gently mix in the buttermilk until a loose dough forms, then turn it onto a floured surface. With floured hands, shape the dough into a round loaf about 6 inches (15 cm) in diameter. Place the loaf on the prepared baking sheet. With a floured knife, cut a shallow X into the center of the loaf. Bake the soda bread for 30 minutes, or until the loaf springs back when touched lightly in the very center.

ABOUT BAKING POWDER AND BAKING SODA

Baking soda and baking powder are used to leaven baked goods, both savory and sweet, such as muffins, biscuits and cookies.

Baking soda is pure sodium bicarbonate and requires an acidic ingredient, such as buttermilk, lemon juice or yogurt, to activate a chemical reaction that produces bubbles and causes baked goods to rise. The reaction begins as soon as the baking soda is moistened, so act quickly and get your baking into the oven as soon as possible. If you don't do this, the rising action will occur in the mixing bowl, not in the oven, which may cause your baked good to deflate and be sunken after cooking.

Baking powder was invented to enable bakers to leaven dough that did not contain an acidic ingredient. It contains baking soda, a drying agent—usually cornstarch—and, most importantly, an acid, such as cream of tartar. With a built-in acidic ingredient it can be used in any baking recipe that needs a lift.

You may wonder why some recipes call for baking powder and baking soda, or why some recipes ask for what some home bakers deem too much baking powder. Baking powder's baking soda content is diluted with other ingredients, so it does not have the same leavening strength as baking soda. That's why in some recipes, particularly those for dense and moist baked goods, a generous amount of baking powder is used or, in some cases, some baking soda is added along with the baking powder.

When using baking powder and baking soda, it's important to whisk them thoroughly into the flour before they are moistened. This will help distribute them equally in the dough and ensure the baked good rises evenly.

If your baking soda or baking powder has been in your cupboard for some time, test it to see if it still works before you use it. To test baking soda, mix ¼ tsp (1 mL) with 2 tsp (10 mL) vinegar. Baking soda that is still good should bubble immediately. To test baking powder, mix 1 tsp (10 mL) with ½ cup (125 mL) hot water. If the baking powder is still good, this mixture should bubble immediately.

ROASTED GARLIC BREAD

Roasting garlic mellows and sweetens its taste and infuses the olive oil it's cooked in with a heavenly flavor. Once the slices of garlic are roasted, they are mashed in the roasting oil and then both are mixed into softened butter, creating a very tasty spread for bread that's then topped with Parmesan cheese and baked. (Pictured on page 190.)

4 garlic cloves, thickly sliced

1½ Tbsp (22.5 mL) extra virgin olive oil

½ cup (125 mL) butter, at room temperature

2 Tbsp (30 mL) chopped fresh parsley

Eight 1-inch (2.5 cm) slices of Italian bread

Freshly grated Parmesan cheese to taste

preparation time •	10 minutes
baking time •	30–32 minu
makes •	8 pieces

ERIC'S OPTIONS
For an even more dynamic-tasting roasted garlic bread, replace the Italian bread with slices of olive bread.

Preheat the oven to 325°F (160°C).

Place the garlic and olive oil in a small baking dish. Cover and roast for 20 minutes, or until the garlic is tender. Transfer the garlic and oil to a bowl. Mash the garlic into small pieces with the back of a small spoon and let it cool to room temperature. Add the butter and parsley to the garlic and oil and mix until well combined.

Increase the oven temperature to 375°F (190°C). Line a baking sheet with parchment paper.

Spread one side of each bread slice with the roasted garlic butter. Set the bread, buttered side up, on the prepared baking sheet. Sprinkle the top of the bread with Parmesan cheese to taste. Bake the roasted garlic bread for 10 to 12 minutes, or until lightly toasted.

BUYING AND STORING GARLIC

There are hundreds of varieties of garlic. Some are quite mild, others are very garlicky and yet others are somewhere in between. If you shop for garlic only at a supermarket, though, you might not know that. Supermarkets usually offer only one type of garlic and it tends to be white-skinned and quite strong tasting.

Look for garlic in season at farmers' markets. There you'll likely find several varieties and you will be able to chat with the grower to determine the one that best suits your palate.

When purchasing, opt for full, heavy-for-their-size bulbs of garlic with firm cloves and dry skins. Store fresh garlic bulbs in an open container in a cool, dark place. They'll keep for 2 months or even longer, depending on their condition when you purchased them.

BUTTERMILK BISCUITS

I like to make these tasty biscuits fairly small by using a 2-inch (5 cm) round cutter. When they're smaller, I don't feel as guilty about having two or three of them! When the dough is ready to transfer to the work surface it will be fairly moist. Don't panic and add more flour. Placed on the floured surface and shaped with your floured hands, the dough will attain the perfect consistency. Serve these biscuits with any of the soups or stews in this book.

preparation time • 20 minutes
baking time • 12–14 minut
makes • 20–24 biscu

ERIC'S OPTIONS
For cheese biscuits, mix 3 oz (90 g) of grated cheddar cheese into the flour mixture before adding the buttermilk. Serve any leftover biscuits with jam and butter for breakfast the next day.

2 cups (500 mL) all-purpose flour

2 tsp (10 mL) baking powder

½ tsp (2.5 mL) baking soda

¼ tsp (1 mL) salt

¼ cup (60 mL) cold butter, cut into small cubes

1 cup (250 mL) buttermilk (see About Buttermilk on page 158)

1 large egg, beaten

Preheat the oven to 425°F (220°C). Line a baking sheet with parchment paper.

Place the flour, baking powder, baking soda and salt in a bowl and whisk to combine. With your fingers, 2 forks or a pastry cutter, work the butter into the flour mixture until thoroughly distributed. Gently mix in the buttermilk until a loose dough forms, then turn it onto a floured surface. With floured hands, shape the dough into a ball, then flatten it into a 1-inch (2.5 cm) thick disk. Cut the dough into 2-inch (5 cm) rounds and place them on the baking sheet. (Gather up the scraps of dough, and press and cut into biscuits as well.) Brush the top of each biscuit lightly with beaten egg. Bake in the middle of the oven for 12 to 14 minutes, or until puffed and golden.

ABOUT BUTTERMILK

In the days when butter was still churned at home, buttermilk was the liquid left behind after the butter was made. It looked kind of like a lighter version of today's skim milk and had a slightly sour taste from the ripe cream used to make the butter.

Today, the buttermilk you see for sale in supermarkets is, of course, made at a commercial dairy. A special bacteria is added to low- or no-fat milk, giving it a slightly thickened texture and tangy flavor.

The acidity in buttermilk makes it an excellent ingredient for quick breads, such as biscuits and scones, as the baking soda often used in these items requires an acidic ingredient to activate it. It can also be used in marinades, such as those for chicken or calamari dishes that get coated in seasoned flour and then fried.

Tangy buttermilk is also great mixed into mashed potatoes, such as Leek and Red Potato Mashers (page 196).

CORNBREAD with PEPPER JACK CHEESE

This moist and marvelous cornbread is spiced up with chili pepper–flavored cheese. It makes a nice side dish for the chili recipes in this book. (Pictured on page 33.)

Soft butter or vegetable oil spray for greasing

1 cup (250 mL) cornmeal

1 cup (250 mL) all-purpose flour

¼ cup (60 mL) sugar

1 Tbsp (15 mL) baking powder

½ tsp (2.5 mL) salt

½ cup (125 mL) grated chili pepper–flavored Monterey Jack cheese (see Note)

1 large egg

1¼ cups (310 mL) buttermilk

¼ cup (60 mL) melted butter

preparation time	•	20 minutes
baking time	•	50 minutes
makes	•	1 loaf

NOTE
Monterey Jack cheese flavored with spicy chilies, such as habañero or jalapeño peppers, is available in the dairy case of many supermarkets.

ERIC'S OPTIONS
If you don't like spicy cheese, use regular Monterey Jack cheese. To help prevent the loaf from sticking to the bottom of the loaf pan, cut a piece of parchment the size of the bottom of the pan. Set the paper in the pan after you've greased it, then spoon in the batter. To make 12 cornbread muffins, divide and spoon the batter into a well-greased 12-cup muffin tin. Bake at 350°F (180°C) for 18 to 20 minutes, or until a muffin springs back when touched very gently in the center.

Preheat the oven to 350°F (180°C). Lightly grease an 8½- × 4½-inch (1.5 L) loaf pan with butter or vegetable oil spray.

Place the cornmeal, flour, sugar, baking powder and salt in a medium bowl and whisk until thoroughly combined. Stir in the cheese.

Break the egg into a clean medium bowl and beat until the yolk and white are well blended. Mix in the buttermilk and melted butter. Add the wet ingredients to the dry and mix until just combined. Spoon the batter into the prepared pan. Bake for 50 minutes, or until the loaf springs back when touched gently in the very center. Cool the loaf on a baking rack for 15 minutes, then turn it out onto a cutting board. Slice the cornbread and enjoy.

ROSEMARY FLATBREAD

Why take the time to make your own flatbread when it is so easy to buy one ready-made? Well, try it once and you'll be surprised not only at how quickly and inexpensively the dough can be made, but also at how wonderful the house smells and the bread tastes.

¾ cup (185 mL) lukewarm (not hot) water

1 tsp (5 mL) instant yeast

½ tsp (2.5 mL) sugar

1½ cups (375 mL) all-purpose flour, plus some for the table and kneading

2 tsp (10 mL) chopped fresh rosemary

¼ tsp (1 mL) salt

1 Tbsp (15 mL) olive oil, plus some for the bowl and baking sheet

Coarse sea salt and coarsely ground black pepper to taste

preparation time	•	**20 minutes***
baking time	•	**18–20 minutes**
makes	•	**1 loaf**

ERIC'S OPTIONS
Instead of fresh rosemary, you could use ½ tsp (2.5 mL) of dried rosemary. Or flavor the dough Indian-style, with ½ tsp (2.5 mL) whole cumin seeds instead of rosemary. Add the cumin when you're asked to add the chopped rosemary. Instead of oil, brush the top of the loaf with 1 Tbsp (15 mL) of melted butter. Sprinkle with salt and pepper as described in the recipe, then bake.

* plus 60 minutes rising time

Place the water, yeast and sugar in a medium bowl and stir to combine. Combine the flour, rosemary and salt in a second medium bowl. Add the wet ingredients to the dry and mix until the dough clumps together loosely. Transfer the dough to a lightly floured surface. Coat your hands with flour and knead until a smooth dough forms, 3 to 4 minutes.

Place the dough in a lightly oiled bowl. Cover tightly and set in a warm, draft-free place. Let the dough rise and double in size, about 1 hour. When the dough has doubled in size, preheat the oven to 450°F (230°C). Lightly oil a nonstick baking sheet.

Set the dough on the prepared baking sheet. Press and stretch the dough into a thin oblong about 10 inches (25 cm) long and 9 inches (23 cm) wide. Brush the top of the dough with the olive oil. Sprinkle with sea salt and pepper. Bake the bread for 18 to 20 minutes, or until puffed and golden.

SEA SALT and OLIVE OIL CRACKERS

These sturdy, quick-baking crackers (pictured on page 5) are great for dunking into soup. You can make these in advance, cool them to room temperature and store them in a tight-sealing container at room temperature for up to 1 week.

preparation time • 20 minutes
baking time • 15–18 minu[...]
makes • 24 crackers

1 cup (250 mL) all-purpose flour

½ tsp (2.5 mL) baking powder

⅓ cup (80 mL) water

3 Tbsp (45 mL) extra virgin olive oil

1–2 tsp (5–10 mL) light (10%) cream

Coarse sea salt to taste

ERIC'S OPTIONS
For added texture, sprinkle these crackers with 2 tsp (10 mL) of sesame seeds before baking. For a cheesy taste, sprinkle 2 Tbsp (30 mL) or so of freshly grated Parmesan cheese on the crackers before baking.

Preheat the oven to 450°F (230°C).

Place the flour and baking powder in a medium bowl and whisk to combine thoroughly. Add the water and olive oil and mix until a loose dough forms. Use your hand to knead the dough in the bowl until smooth.

Set a 12-inch (30 cm) wide, 16-inch (40 cm) long piece of parchment paper on a work surface. Set the dough in the center of the paper and flatten it into a thick disk. Set a piece of parchment paper, the same size as the first, on top of the dough. With a rolling pin, roll the dough into a thin rectangle about 8 inches (20 cm) wide and 12 inches (30 cm) long. (The dough does not have to be perfectly rectangular.)

Remove the top piece of parchment. Lift the bottom sheet of paper by its sides and set it and the dough on a baking sheet. Cut the dough in half lengthwise. Now cut the dough into 12 slices widthwise. You should have 24 rectangles of dough.

Brush the top of each cracker lightly with cream and sprinkle with sea salt to taste. Bake the crackers for 15 to 18 minutes, or until crisp and golden. Set the pan of crackers on a baking rack and cool to room temperature.

SALADS AND CONDIMENTS

BUTTER LETTUCE SALAD with WALNUTS and DRIED CHERRIES

This is a light, palate-refreshing salad that I like to serve before or alongside rich-tasting entrées, such as Slow-Simmered French-Style Beans with Confit Duck Leg (pictured; recipe page 93).

preparation time • 10 minutes
cooking time • none
makes • 6 servings

1½ Tbsp (22.5 mL) raspberry vinegar

2 tsp (10 mL) Dijon mustard

1 tsp (5 mL) chopped fresh tarragon, or pinch dried

¼ tsp (1 mL) honey

¼ cup (60 mL) extra virgin olive oil

Salt and freshly ground black pepper to taste

1 large head butter lettuce, stems trimmed, head separated
   into individual leaves

⅓–½ cup (80–125 mL) walnut halves

⅓–½ cup (80–125 mL) dried cherries

ERIC'S OPTIONS
Dried cherries are sold at specialty food stores and some supermarkets, often in the bulk foods section. If you can't find them, use dried cranberries, which are more widely available, instead.

Combine the vinegar, mustard, tarragon and honey in a salad bowl. Slowly whisk in the oil, then season with salt and pepper. Add the lettuce and gently toss to coat with the vinaigrette. Mound the lettuce on 6 salad plates. Top with the walnuts and cherries and serve.

Read "About Vinaigrette" on page 166 . . .

ABOUT VINAIGRETTE

Vinaigrette is a tangy mix of oil and vinegar, traditionally in a 3:1 ratio. However, this ratio can change depending on the vinegar's tartness. For example, if you use slightly sweet balsamic vinegar, you will need less oil. If you use very strong, everyday white vinegar, you might need more oil to counter its sharpness. Lemon juice or another acidic ingredient sometimes replaces the vinegar.

Herbs, garlic and spices are often added to a vinaigrette to boost its flavor. Dijon mustard is also often added to vinaigrette for flavoring and to act as an emulsifier that holds the oil and vinegar together when blended.

There are many ready-to-use, commercially made, bottled vinaigrette salad dressings available in supermarkets. I'm not a fan of them, because one of the main ingredients is often water, which is not something you'll ever whisk into a homemade vinaigrette unless you want to dilute its fine taste. If you need to store your homemade vinaigrette, place it in a tight-sealing jar in the refrigerator for up to 1 week. Shake well before using.

SWEET and TANGY SIX-VEGETABLE COLESLAW

I enjoy coleslaw and I like it even better when I make it with a nutritious mix of vegetables, such as the recipe below (pictured on page 112). Serve this alongside some of the diner-style entrées in this book, such as Pulled Pork Sandwiches (page 113).

preparation time	•	**20 minutes**
cooking time	•	**none**
makes	•	**8 servings**

ERIC'S OPTIONS
Instead of green cabbage, use red cabbage, or try a mix of both green and red cabbage.

3 Tbsp (45 mL) cider vinegar

1 Tbsp (15 mL) honey

2 tsp (10 mL) Dijon mustard

Salt and freshly ground black pepper to taste

2 Tbsp (30 mL) vegetable oil

4 cups (1 L) finely shredded cabbage (about ½ small head)

1 cup (250 mL) coarsely grated carrot

1 cup (250 mL) coarsely grated yellow or green zucchini

6 radishes, halved and thinly sliced

3–4 green onions, thinly sliced

1 small red bell pepper, cut into small cubes

Place the vinegar, honey, mustard and salt and pepper in a large bowl. Slowly whisk in the oil. Toss in the remaining ingredients.

ABOUT COLESLAW

The word "coleslaw" is derived from the Dutch word *koolsla*, which is formed from *kool*, meaning cabbage, and *sla*, meaning salad. Dutch immigrants brought this salad to North America and its popularity quickly spread.

Opt for cabbage with a tightly packed head and bright, sturdy leaves. It will give you crisp and almost juicy shredded cabbage. No matter how fresh the cabbage is, the longer dressed coleslaw sits, the less crisp it becomes.

ROMAINE HEARTS with FOCACCIA CROUTONS and PARMESAN

This caesar-like salad is made with romaine hearts, the crisp, center portion of romaine lettuce, sold in bags in the produce section of most supermarkets. I like to serve this salad with Italian-style entrées, such as Veal Meatballs in Tomato Sauce with Fresh Basil (page 137).

preparation time • 20 minutes
cooking time • 8–10 minutes
makes • 4 servings

8 thin slices focaccia bread

½ cup (125 mL) mayonnaise

⅓ cup (80 mL) freshly grated Parmesan cheese, plus some for sprinkling

⅓ cup (80 mL) buttermilk

1 Tbsp (15 mL) fresh lemon juice

1 tsp (5 mL) sugar

1 garlic clove, minced

Salt and freshly ground black pepper to taste

Splash Tabasco sauce

Splash Worcestershire sauce

2 romaine hearts, chopped, washed and dried

4 lemon wedges

ERIC'S OPTIONS
Instead of slicing the focaccia bread, make more traditional croutons by cutting the bread into small cubes. Toast them on the baking sheet as directed for the focaccia slices. Sprinkle the toasted bread cubes over the salad when ready to serve. If you like anchovies, you could mix 1 tsp (5 mL) of anchovy paste into the salad dressing.

Preheat the oven to 350°F (180°C). Line a baking sheet with parchment paper. Set the focaccia slices on the prepared baking sheet. Bake for 8 to 10 minutes, or until lightly toasted. Remove from the oven and set aside.

Combine the mayonnaise, Parmesan cheese, buttermilk, lemon juice, sugar, garlic, salt, pepper, Tabasco and Worcestershire sauce in a small bowl. Divide the romaine hearts among 4 salad plates. Drizzle some of the dressing overtop and serve the rest tableside. Set 2 croutons alongside each salad. Garnish each salad with a lemon wedge, sprinkle with a little Parmesan cheese and serve.

ASIAN-STYLE CUCUMBER and PEANUT SALAD

I like to serve this salad alongside spicy dishes, such as the slow cooker curries you'll find in this book. It's refreshing and will help cool down your palate if you made the curry extra spicy.

¼ **cup (60 mL)** fresh lime juice

1 **Tbsp (15 mL)** sugar

1 **Tbsp (15 mL)** vegetable oil

2 **tsp (10 mL)** peeled, finely grated fresh ginger (see About Fresh Ginger on page 30)

2 medium shallots, finely chopped

1 medium English cucumber, thinly sliced

½ **cup (125 mL)** unsalted roasted peanuts, coarsely chopped

¼ **cup (60 mL)** chopped fresh cilantro

preparation time	•	15 minutes
cooking time	•	none
makes	•	6 servings

ERIC'S OPTIONS
Make cucumber and cashew salad by replacing the peanuts with coarsely chopped unsalted roasted cashews. If you don't care for cilantro, replace it with chopped fresh mint or green onion.

Place the lime juice, sugar, oil and ginger in a medium bowl and whisk to combine. Add the remaining ingredients and toss to combine again. Let the flavors meld at room temperature for 10 minutes. Gently toss the salad again and serve.

WHEN I LEARNED TO LOVE CILANTRO

People seem to be divided about cilantro: they either love it or hate it. I was in the hate camp for quite some time, wary of even trying what I considered a medicinal, soapy-tasting herb.

That started to change in my late 20s, when I began frequenting a popular Vietnamese restaurant in Toronto. Friends told me I had to try a dish listed as Number 25. It consisted of two crisp and divine-tasting spring rolls set atop a bowl of cool noodles and accompanied by a sweet-and-sour–tasting sauce spiked with chilies, grated carrot, bean sprouts and green onion.

However, there was one more ingredient in the sauce that I somehow missed. You guessed it! Cilantro. The dish looked so good I dove in with abandon before thinking, "Hey, wait a minute!" But as I kept eating I discovered that the cilantro, of which there was actually only a modest amount, really worked with the other flavors in the dish. From that moment on I changed from being a cilantro hater to a cilantro lover.

My experience explains why some culinary guides advise cooks to use cilantro with discretion. People who are unaccustomed to its flavor—such as me, way back when—may find it unappealing if used too generously. This is good advice if you want to introduce someone to the wide range of inviting dishes to which cilantro can be added. Check out the curries, the chilies and some of the soups in this book to begin the conversion process.

NEW RED and WHITE POTATO SALAD

This tangy potato salad is made without mayonnaise and can be enjoyed hot or at room temperature. That means you can get it straight on the table once it's made as there's no prechilling required. It makes a nice side dish for Shredded Beef Sandwiches (page 136).

preparation time • 10 minutes
cooking time • 10 minutes
makes • 8 servings

ERIC'S OPTIONS

I like to use a mix of red and white potatoes in this recipe because it adds visual interest. If desired, you could, of course, use only white or red potatoes.

¾ lb (375 g) red-skinned potatoes (unpeeled), cubed

¾ lb (375 g) white-skinned potatoes (unpeeled), cubed

3 Tbsp (45 mL) white wine vinegar

3 Tbsp (45 mL) olive oil

2 Tbsp (30 mL) Dijon mustard

Salt and freshly ground black pepper to taste

Pinch sugar

2–3 green onions, thinly sliced

1 small carrot, grated

1 large celery stalk, diced

Boil the potatoes until just tender, about 10 minutes. While the potatoes cook, place the vinegar, oil, mustard, salt, pepper and sugar in a large bowl and mix to combine.

When the potatoes are cooked, drain them well and add them plus the green onion, carrot and celery to the bowl, and toss to combine. Serve hot or at room temperature.

FRESH MINT CHUTNEY

This rich green, intensely flavored chutney can be used to accent savory dishes that might benefit from having a spicy hit of mint alongside, such as Lamb Curry with Potatoes and Peas (page 146).

preparation time • 25 minutes
cooking time • none
makes • 1 cup (250 mL)

1 cup (250 mL) fresh mint leaves, packed

3 green onions, thinly sliced

1 small, fresh green serrano chili, coarsely chopped including seeds

1 garlic clove, minced

¼ cup (60 mL) fresh lime juice

2 Tbsp (30 mL) vegetable oil

2 Tbsp (30 mL) water

1 Tbsp (15 mL) sugar

½ tsp (2.5 mL) ground cumin

½ tsp (2.5 mL) salt

ERIC'S OPTIONS
Make cilantro chutney by replacing the mint with cilantro leaves.

Place all the ingredients in a food processor and pulse until well combined and finely chopped. Transfer to a serving bowl. Cover and let the flavors meld for 20 minutes or so before mixing again and serving. Store any leftover chutney in a tight-sealing jar in the refrigerator. It will keep for 2 to 3 days and can be used to flavor any leftover curry or other dishes, such as grilled meat or fish.

PICKLED BEETS with BALSAMIC and SPICE

Sweet-and-sour-tasting beets are made dark and inviting by canning them with balsamic vinegar. Make these in summer or fall and you'll have plenty of homemade pickled beets to enjoy during the long winter months, particularly if you make a double batch. (Pictured on page 91.)

5 lb (2.2 kg) beets without tops

2¼ cups (560 mL) sugar

2¾ cups (685 mL) water for pickling mixture

1¾ cups (435 mL) white vinegar

¾ cup (185 mL) balsamic vinegar

2 Tbsp (30 mL) pickling spice

preparation time • 40 minutes
cooking time • 50–60 minu
makes • six 2-cup
(500 mL) ja

ERIC'S OPTIONS
To make raspberry-flavored beets, replace the balsamic vinegar with an equal amount of raspberry vinegar.

Place the beets, unpeeled, in a pot and cover completely with cold water. Gently boil them until tender, 30 to 40 minutes, depending on their size. Drain the beets, cool them in ice-cold water and drain them again.

Sterilize six 2-cup (500 mL) canning jars in boiling water for 10 minutes.

Meanwhile, peel the beets. The skins should just slip off in your fingers. Trim off the rough top part from each beet with a small knife and cut each beet into wedges or ¼- to ½-inch (6 mm to 1 cm) thick slices.

Pack the beets into the sterilized jars. Sterilize 6 snap-top canning jar lids in boiling water for 5 minutes. While the lids boil, place the sugar, water, vinegars and pickling spice in a pot. Bring to a boil. Boil, stirring to dissolve the sugar, for about 3 minutes. Carefully pour this mixture over the beets, leaving a ½-inch (1 cm) headspace at the top of each jar. Wipe the rims clean, then top each jar with a lid. Set on the jars' screwbands and turn just until fingertip-tight.

Heat-process the jars of beets in boiling water for 15 minutes. Set them on a rack to cool at room temperature for 24 hours. Check the seal. A properly sealed lid will be concave (curve downward). Label and date the beets and store in a cool, dark place. Refrigerate after opening.

WHY HEAT-PROCESS PRESERVES?

Modern canning guides advise you to heat-process homemade canned foods, such as preserves, pickles and condiments, in boiling water or a pressure canner to inactivate enzymes, yeasts and other microorganisms. During heat-processing the canning jar is heated and its contents expand. Changes of internal pressure vent gases or air from the jar that, after processing, cause the atmospheric pressure outside the jar to be greater than inside. This causes the canning jar's lid to be pulled downward, creating a vacuum seal that prevents contaminants from entering the food. How long you heat-process will be determined by what you are canning and should be specified in the recipe.

ROASTED RED PEPPER AIOLI

Aioli is a garlic-rich mayonnaise that originated in Provence, France. The roasted red pepper blended into this version gives it a greater depth of flavor and a pinkish-red color. I like to use this as a spread for sandwiches or a dip for raw vegetables, and for dolloping onto seafood stews, such as Mediterranean-Style Seafood Stew (pictured; page 58).

1 large roasted red pepper, thickly sliced (see Eric's Options)

¾ cup (185 mL) mayonnaise

1–2 garlic cloves, minced

2 Tbsp (30 mL) coarsely chopped fresh parsley

1 Tbsp (15 mL) fresh lemon juice

½ tsp (2.5 mL) finely grated lemon zest

Salt and freshly ground black pepper to taste

Place all the ingredients in a food processor and pulse until smooth. (You could also use an immersion blender if it has a vessel designed for blending things in.) Transfer the aioli to a bowl, cover and refrigerate until needed.

preparation time •	5 minutes
cooking time •	none
makes •	1¼ cups (310 mL)

ERIC'S OPTIONS

Roasted red peppers are sold at most supermarkets in jars or tubs, or in bulk in the deli section. If you want to roast your own red pepper, place a large red bell pepper in a small baking pan lined with parchment paper. Roast at 375°F (190°C) for 30 minutes, turning once or twice, or until the skin is blistered. Remove the pan from the oven and cover with foil. Let the pepper sit for 20 minutes. Uncover the pepper and slip off the skin. Cut the pepper in half and remove the seeds, and it's ready to use.

MANGO CHUTNEY

This colorful and lively sweet-and-sour chutney (pictured on page 76) makes a nice, fresh condiment to serve alongside a curry such as Green Thai Curry Chicken Thighs (page 77).

1 cup finely cubed ripe mango

1 small ripe tomato, finely chopped

2 Tbsp (30 mL) finely chopped onion

2 Tbsp (30 mL) chopped fresh cilantro

1 Tbsp (15 mL) fresh lime juice, or to taste

1 tsp (5 mL) sugar

Salt to taste

preparation time • 10 minutes
cooking time • none
makes • 1½ cups (375 mL)

ERIC'S OPTIONS
Make fresh papaya chutney by replacing the mango with cubes of papaya. For spicy chutney, add crushed chili flakes to taste.

Place all the ingredients in a medium bowl and toss to combine. Cover and refrigerate until needed. This can be made several hours before serving, but it is at its best when served soon after making, when all the ingredients will be at their freshest.

ABOUT FRESH MANGOES

When purchasing mangoes, choose those with smooth, taut skin. A ripe mango has a heavenly tropical fruit aroma and the flesh under the skin yields slightly to gentle pressure. If a mango is unripe, simply leave it out at room temperature for a few days to ripen, as you would a banana. If you want to speed up the ripening process, place the mango in a paper bag. Ripe mangoes can be stored in the refrigerator for up to a week. Mangoes contain vitamins A, C and D and are a source of fiber and potassium, among other things.

RICE AND PASTA

JASMINE FRIED RICE

Jasmine rice is a long-grain rice variety native to Thailand but now grown in other parts of the world, such as the southern United States. Its name comes from the wonderful aroma—similar to the scent of jasmine flowers—it exudes when it's being cooked. That is why the rice is also sometimes referred to as "fragrant rice." (Pictured on page 76.)

preparation time • 15 minutes
cooking time • 6–7 minutes
makes • 4 servings

2 Tbsp (30 mL) vegetable oil

1 celery stalk, finely chopped

½ small onion, finely chopped

½ cup (125 mL) grated carrot

1 garlic clove, finely chopped

3 cups (750 mL) cooked jasmine rice, cold

3 Tbsp (45 mL) fresh lime juice

2 Tbsp (30 mL) fish sauce (see Note)

2 Tbsp (30 mL) golden brown sugar

½ tsp (2.5 mL) hot Asian-style chili sauce

¾ cup (185 mL) frozen peas

¼ cup (60 mL) chopped fresh basil

NOTE
Fish sauce is a salty liquid made from salted, fermented fish. It is used as a seasoning in some Asian cuisines, such as Thai and Vietnamese. You'll find it in the Asian food aisle of most supermarkets and at Asian food stores.

ERIC'S OPTIONS
The fried rice could be made with regular long-grain rice if that's what you have on hand, although it won't be as deliciously aromatic. If you don't care for fish sauce, substitute another liquid, such as light soy sauce.

Place the oil in a wok or large skillet set over medium-high heat. When hot, add the celery, onion, carrot and garlic and stir-fry for 2 minutes. Add the rice and stir-fry for 2 to 3 minutes more. Mix in the lime juice, fish sauce, brown sugar and chili sauce, and stir-fry for 1 minute more. Mix in the peas and basil, cook for 1 minute more and serve.

TIPS FOR MAKING FRIED RICE

Do not use freshly cooked, hot rice to make fried rice because it can overcook during frying, turn mushy and clump together. If you want to make fried rice, plan ahead and cook and cool the rice a day or two beforehand.

To make 3 cups (750 mL) of cooked rice, the amount called for in this book's recipes, place 1¼ cups (310 mL) of long-grain white or jasmine rice in a pot and pour in 1¾ cups (435 mL) cold water. Bring the rice to a boil over high heat, reduce the heat to its lowest setting, cover and steam the rice, undisturbed, for 15 to 18 minutes, or until just tender. Spoon the rice into a wide, shallow dish, fluff with a fork, cool to room temperature and cover and refrigerate.

Before you fry the rice, allow the cold rice to sit out at room temperature for about 20 minutes. This step will help the grains to separate more easily once you start to fry them.

When cooking fried rice, make sure your wok or skillet is hot. This will ensure the rice actually does fry and takes on the slightly smoky taste good fried rice should have. When stir-frying rice, use a neutral-tasting oil with a high smoke point (the highest temperature it can reach before it burns), such as peanut, corn or vegetable oil.

CASHEW FRIED RICE

The cashews that so richly flavor this rice can be expensive. If that's a concern, buy them from a bulk food store or a supermarket that sells bulk foods. That way you can buy only the exact amount required for this recipe with no waste.

2 Tbsp (30 mL) vegetable oil

1 cup (250 mL) finely chopped green cabbage

1 small carrot, quartered lengthwise and thinly sliced

½ medium onion, finely chopped

1 garlic clove, minced

3 cups (750 mL) cooked long-grain white or brown rice
(see Tips for Making Fried Rice on page 181), cold

¾ cup (185 mL) unsalted roasted cashews

½ cup (125 mL) frozen peas

2 Tbsp (30 mL) soy sauce

2 green onions, thinly sliced

Freshly ground black pepper to taste

preparation time • **10 minutes**
cooking time • **6–7 minutes**
makes • **4 servings**

ERIC'S OPTIONS
Instead of cashews, use unsalted roasted peanuts or whole almonds in this recipe. Instead of green cabbage, use 1 cup (250 mL) of finely chopped napa or Chinese cabbage.

Place the oil in a wok or large skillet set over medium-high heat. Add the cabbage, carrot, onion and garlic and stir-fry for 2 minutes. Add the rice and stir-fry for 2 to 3 minutes more. Mix in the remaining ingredients and stir-fry for 2 minutes, or until the rice is heated through.

RICE PILAF with THYME, LEMON and GARLIC

Pilaf is the name given to any number of rice dishes tastily flavored during cooking. In this case, minced fresh thyme, lemon zest and juice, garlic and stock accomplish that goal.

preparation time • 10 minutes
cooking time • 18–21 minutes
makes • 4 servings

1 Tbsp (15 mL) olive oil

1 medium shallot, finely chopped

1 garlic clove, minced

1 cup (250 mL) long-grain white rice

1½ cups (375 mL) chicken or vegetable stock

1 Tbsp (15 mL) fresh lemon juice

2 tsp (10 mL) minced fresh thyme

2 tsp (10 mL) finely grated lemon zest

Salt and white pepper to taste

ERIC'S OPTIONS
Instead of thyme, use fresh tarragon. In place of lemon zest and juice, use orange zest and juice, or use a mix of citrus zest and juice.

Place the oil in a small- to medium-sized pot set over medium to medium-high heat. Add the shallot and garlic and cook until softened, about 1 minute. Mix in the rice and cook for 2 minutes more. Stir in the remaining ingredients and bring to a boil. Cover, reduce the heat to its lowest setting and cook, undisturbed, for 15 to 18 minutes, or until the rice is tender. Fluff the rice with a fork and serve.

MIXED VEGETABLE RICE PILAF

This rice dish contains a mix of five vegetables. Some, such as the garlic and onion, are used more for flavoring. Others, such as the carrot, red bell pepper and green peas, also add flavor but are included more for their attractive color.

preparation time	•	10 minutes
cooking time	•	20–23 minu‹
makes	•	4 servings

1 Tbsp (15 mL) vegetable oil

½ small onion, finely chopped

1 cup (250 mL) long-grain white rice

1 garlic clove, minced

¼ tsp (1 mL) dried oregano

1¾ cups (435 mL) chicken or vegetable stock

½ small red bell pepper, finely diced

⅓ cup (80 mL) grated carrot

Salt and white pepper to taste

⅓ cup (80 mL) frozen peas

ERIC'S OPTIONS
Instead of white rice, use brown rice and increase the stock by ¼ cup (60 mL). After the rice comes to a boil, cover it and reduce the heat to its lowest setting. Cook the brown rice, undisturbed, for 35 minutes, or until tender.

Heat the oil in a small- to medium-sized pot set over medium to medium-high heat. Add the onion and cook until tender, about 3 minutes. Mix in the rice, garlic and oregano and cook for 2 minutes more. Mix in the stock, red pepper, grated carrot and salt and pepper and bring to a boil. Cover, reduce the heat to its lowest setting and cook, undisturbed, for 15 to 18 minutes, or until the rice is tender. Fluff the rice with a fork, mix in the peas and heat them through for a minute or so, then serve.

SAFFRON RICE with PARSLEY

Saffron is dried stigmas of a small flower called the purple crocus (*Crocus sativus*). It is also the world's most expensive spice. More than fourteen thousand stigmas are required to make 1 ounce (30 g) of saffron. Luckily, a little goes a long way in turning the rice in this recipe into an attractive, golden-hued side dish flecked with vibrant green parsley. If you don't use saffron very often, it's actually fairly affordable. You can usually buy it in small containers, enough for three to four recipes, for under $10.

preparation time • 5 minutes
cooking time • 27–30 minutes
makes • 4 servings

ERIC'S OPTIONS
Instead of parsley, accent the rice with another type of fresh herb, such as snipped chives.

½ tsp (2.5 mL) loosely packed saffron threads, crumbled

1 Tbsp (15 mL) olive oil

1 medium shallot, finely chopped

1 cup (250 mL) long-grain white rice

1½ cups (375 mL) chicken or vegetable stock

Salt and ground white pepper to taste

2 Tbsp (30 mL) chopped fresh parsley

Steep the saffron in 2 Tbsp (30 mL) of boiling water for 10 minutes. Heat the oil in a small- to medium-sized pot set over medium to medium-high heat. Add the shallot and cook for 1 minute. Add the rice and cook, stirring, for 1 minute more. Add the steeped saffron and its liquid, stock and salt and pepper. Bring to a rapid boil, then cover, reduce the heat to its lowest setting and cook, undisturbed, for 15 to 18 minutes, or until the rice is tender. Fluff the rice with a fork, mix in the parsley and serve.

SPANISH-STYLE BROWN RICE

This is a homemade version of the spiced rice dish served in many Mexican restaurants in Canada and the United States. What sets this apart is that, instead of white rice, nutritious, almost nutty-tasting brown rice is used to make it.

3 Tbsp (45 mL) olive oil

1 medium green bell pepper, finely chopped

½ medium onion, finely chopped

2 garlic cloves, minced

1½ cups (375 mL) long-grain brown rice (see About Brown Rice on facing page)

1½ tsp (7.5 mL) ground cumin

1½ tsp (7.5 mL) chili powder

⅛ tsp (0.5 mL) cayenne pepper

3 cups (750 mL) chicken or vegetable stock

preparation time • 10 minutes
cooking time • 40 minutes
makes • 6 servings

ERIC'S OPTIONS
If you would prefer to use white long-grain rice to make this dish, reduce the amount of stock to 2¾ cups (685 mL). After the rice comes to a boil, cover it and reduce the heat to its lowest setting. Cook the rice, undisturbed, for only 15 to 18 minutes, or until tender.

Pour the oil into a medium-sized pot and set over medium to medium-high heat. Add the bell pepper, onion and garlic and cook for 3 minutes. Add the rice, cumin, chili powder and cayenne and cook for 2 minutes more. Pour in the stock, increase the heat to high and bring to a rapid boil. Cover, reduce the heat to its lowest setting and cook, undisturbed, for 35 minutes, or until the rice is tender. Fluff the rice with a fork and serve.

ABOUT BROWN RICE

Brown rice has kernels of the grain that, unlike white rice, have only the hull removed. This leaves the tan-colored bran layer intact and preserves the nutritious elements it contains, such as vitamins B and E, calcium, protein, thiamine, niacin, riboflavin and iron. Because of the protective bran layer, brown rice takes about twice as long to cook as white rice and has a chewier texture.

Brown rice is available in short-, medium- and long-grain varieties. Asian-style rice varieties such as jasmine and basmati are also available in a brown format. Because the oil-rich bran is still intact, brown rice can go rancid more quickly than white rice. Store brown rice in a tight-sealing container in a cool, dark place or in the refrigerator and buy only what you can use within a month or two.

SAFFRON RISOTTO

As the rice cooks in the stock and is stirred frequently, its starches release into the liquid. This creates an almost creamy sauce around the rice that in this case turns a lovely golden color thanks to the saffron. This risotto is the perfect side dish to serve with Osso Bucco with Gremolata (page 138).

½ tsp (2.5 mL) loosely packed saffron threads, crumbled

6 cups (1.5 L) chicken stock

3 Tbsp (45 mL) olive oil

½ medium onion, finely chopped

1½ cups (375 mL) risotto rice (see Rice for Risotto on facing page)

½ cup (125 mL) dry white wine

½ cup (125 mL) freshly grated Parmesan cheese

2 Tbsp (30 mL) chopped fresh parsley

Salt and freshly ground pepper to taste

preparation time • 5 minutes
cooking time • 40 minutes
makes • 4–6 serving

ERIC'S OPTIONS
If you don't wish to use or don't have any saffron, prepare this recipe without it to make risotto bianco, or white risotto.

Steep the saffron in 2 Tbsp (30 mL) of boiling water for 10 minutes. Place the stock in a pot and bring to just below a simmer over medium-high heat. When there, reduce the heat to its lowest setting and keep the stock warm on the stove.

Heat the oil in a medium-sized pot set over medium to medium-high heat. Add the onion and cook until tender, about 3 minutes. Add the rice and cook, stirring, until it has a nutty, toasted aroma, about 2 minutes. Add the wine and the saffron and its liquid. Adjust the heat to bring to a gentle simmer. Cook until the wine is almost fully absorbed by the rice.

Add 1 cup (250 mL) of the stock, stir and cook until it is almost fully absorbed by the rice. Add the remaining stock ½ cup to 1 cup (125 to 250 mL) at a time, cooking and stirring until it is almost fully absorbed by the rice before adding the next portion. Continue doing this until the rice is tender. You may not need all the stock.

When done, the rice should be al dente, tender with some bite. The texture of the risotto should be a creamy mass with enough body to stand up slightly when scooped into a bowl or plate.

When the rice is tender, remove it from the heat and stir in the Parmesan cheese, parsley and salt and pepper. Cover and let sit for a few minutes before serving.

RICE FOR RISOTTO

The best types of rice to use for risotto are stubby, short- or medium-grained varieties. They have a high starch content and absorb less liquid so that when cooked, the rice maintains a nice texture, and the almost creamy sauce that risotto is famous for is created around it. You'll find these types of rice for sale at many supermarkets. Sometimes they are simply labeled "risotto rice." You'll also find specific varieties of rice, particularly in specialty food stores, that are excellent for making risotto: arborio, carnaroli or vialone nano, for example.

SPAGHETTI with LEMON, CHILIES and GARLIC

This pasta is perked up with the palate-stimulating tastes of lemon, chilies and garlic. The spaghetti makes a nice side dish to serve with some of the saucy Italian-style entrées in this book, such as Veal Meatballs in Tomato Sauce with Fresh Basil (pictured; recipe page 137).

preparation time • 5 minutes
cooking time • 10 minutes
makes • 4 servings

¾ lb (375 g) spaghetti

2 Tbsp (30 mL) butter

2 Tbsp (30 mL) olive oil

3–4 garlic cloves, minced

¼ tsp (1 mL) crushed chili flakes, or to taste

½ cup (125 mL) chicken or vegetable stock

2 tsp (10 mL) finely grated lemon zest

3 Tbsp (45 mL) chopped fresh parsley

Salt to taste

ERIC'S OPTIONS
Instead of spaghetti, try another long noodle in this recipe, such as fettuccini, linguini or spaghettini. Instead of parsley, try another herb, such as chopped fresh oregano or basil.

Cook the spaghetti until tender in a large pot of lightly salted, boiling water, about 8 minutes. While the spaghetti cooks, place the butter and oil in a large skillet set over medium heat. When the butter is melted, add the garlic and chili flakes and cook until fragrant, about 1 minute. Add the stock and lemon zest and bring to a simmer. When the pasta is cooked, drain it well, reserving ½ cup (125 mL) of its cooking liquid. Add the spaghetti, reserved cooking liquid, parsley and salt to the skillet, toss to combine and serve.

ORZO with BASIL and PARMESAN CHEESE

Orzo is a small, rice-shaped pasta that tastily absorbs the flavor of the ingredients it's combined with, which in this case include olive oil, freshly grated Parmesan cheese and fresh basil. The orzo could be served alongside a number of the Mediterranean-style entrées in this book, such as Lamb Shanks Braised with Wine, Citrus and Spice (page 148).

1½ cups (375 mL) orzo

½ cup (125 mL) freshly grated Parmesan cheese

¼ cup (60 mL) chopped fresh basil

2 Tbsp (30 mL) olive oil

Salt and freshly ground black pepper to taste

preparation time	•	5 minutes
cooking time	•	7–8 minutes
makes	•	4 servings

ERIC'S OPTIONS
Any leftover orzo could be turned into a cold salad. Simply mix some raw, cut vegetables, such as green bell pepper, cherry tomatoes and carrot, into the orzo, drizzle with lemon juice and olive oil and serve.

Cook the orzo in boiling, lightly salted water until just tender, 7 to 8 minutes. While it cooks, place the cheese, basil and oil in a medium serving bowl.

When cooked, drain the orzo well, reserving ¼ cup (60 mL) of the cooking liquid. Add the orzo, reserved cooking liquid and salt and pepper to the serving bowl. Toss everything to combine and serve.

POTATOES AND VEGETABLES

GARLIC MASHED YUKON GOLD POTATOES with KALE

This earthy-tasting mash (pictured on page 53) is flecked with nutritious kale, a source of vitamins A and C, calcium, fiber, folic acid and iron. In the wintertime, when I'm in the mood for comfort food, I like to serve this as a side dish for a rich and saucy entrée, such as Lamb Stew with Leeks and Guinness (page 144).

6 fresh kale leaves, washed well, tough lower stems trimmed (see Buying and Handling Kale on facing page)

¾ **cup (185 mL)** chicken or vegetable stock

1½ **lb (750 g)** Yukon Gold potatoes, peeled and quartered

4 large garlic cloves, thickly sliced

2 **Tbsp (30 mL)** melted butter

Salt and white pepper to taste

preparation time • **15 minutes**
cooking time • **21–24 minu**
makes • **4 servings**

ERIC'S OPTIONS
Although Yukon Gold potatoes will give this mash a light yellow color that looks good with the rich green kale, you could use baking or russet potatoes if that's what you have on hand.

Cut the kale leaves in half lengthwise. Now cut the half leaves widthwise, into ¼-inch (6 mm) strips. Bring the stock to a simmer in a wide skillet. Add the kale and cook until just tender, 3 to 4 minutes. Remove the kale from the heat and set aside in its cooking liquid.

Place the potatoes and garlic in a pot, cover with cold water by at least 2 inches (5 cm) and bring to a boil over medium-high heat. Reduce the heat and simmer gently until very tender, 18 to 20 minutes.

Drain the potatoes well, ensuring the garlic stays in the pot. Thoroughly mash the potatoes and garlic as smooth as possible. Mix in the melted butter, reserved kale and its cooking liquid, and salt and pepper. Serve.

BUYING AND HANDLING KALE

There are many varieties of kale, but the bunches you'll see for sale at supermarkets will most often have deep green leaves tinged with shades of purple or blue. When buying, opt for crisp-looking bunches with, preferably, smaller, more tender leaves. Steer clear of kale with leaves that are limp or yellowing.

Kale is fairly perishable, but if you need to store it for a few days, wrap it, unwashed, in a damp paper towel, place it in a plastic bag and store in your refrigerator crisper. To prepare the kale for eating raw or for cooking, thoroughly wash the leaves in cold water. The stems can be eaten, but if they are overly tough, they should be trimmed off.

LEEK and RED POTATO MASHERS

This inviting side dish has appealing red and green colors. The red potatoes in this recipe are a waxy variety that can become gummy in texture if you mash them vigorously. (See Tips for Making Mashed Potatoes on page 199.)

1½ lb (750 g) medium red-skinned potatoes (unpeeled), quartered

2 Tbsp (30 mL) butter

1 small leek, white and pale green part only, cut lengthwise in half, thoroughly washed and thinly sliced (see About Leeks on facing page)

¼ cup (60 mL) chicken stock

⅓–½ cup (80–125 mL) buttermilk

Salt and freshly ground black pepper to taste

preparation time •	15 minutes
cooking time •	20 minutes
makes •	4 servings

ERIC'S OPTIONS
If you don't care for the tangy taste of buttermilk, you can use regular milk in these potatoes. For an additional hit of color, mix 1 Tbsp (15 mL) of chopped fresh parsley into the potatoes when adding the leek.

Place the potatoes in a pot, cover with cold water by at least 2 inches (5 cm) and bring to a boil over medium-high heat. Reduce the heat until the potatoes simmer gently. Simmer until very tender, about 15 minutes.

While the potatoes are cooking, melt the butter in a skillet set over medium to medium-high heat. Add the leek and cook for 3 to 4 minutes. Add the stock, bring to a simmer and cook until the stock has almost evaporated and the leek is very tender, 4 to 5 minutes. Remove from the heat.

When the potatoes are tender, drain them well and mash them. Mix in the buttermilk, reserved leek and any liquid in the skillet, and salt and pepper. Serve.

ABOUT LEEKS

Despite leeks' family connections—they are related to both garlic and onion and have a taste somewhere between the two—they are fairly mild in flavor and aroma. That quality makes them a more refined ingredient to use in a wide range of dishes, such as a creamy soup, quiche, stew or potato dish.

When buying leeks, choose unblemished, firm leeks with vibrant-looking green and white portions. Store them in a plastic bag in your refrigerator crisper. Very fresh leeks will last for up to 5 days.

Very small, young leeks, sometimes called baby leeks, can be cooked whole and served as a hot or cold vegetable side dish. Wash them well before using. Supermarkets generally sell medium to large leeks. The multiple layers in the white portion of these larger leeks trap dirt, so it is crucial to wash them before using. Simply trim off the hairy root end and cut the leek in half lengthwise, which exposes the places where dirt can get trapped. Wash away any dirt and dry the leek, and it's ready to be chopped or sliced.

ROQUEFORT and CHIVE MASHED POTATOES

Blue cheese lovers will adore these ultrarich mashed potatoes (pictured on page 123) strewn with small nuggets of Roquefort. Roquefort is one of France's most famous cheeses and French law says that only cheese aged in natural caves near Roquefort-sur-Soulzon, the birthplace of this cheese, can use that name.

2½ lb (1.25 kg) russet or baking potatoes, peeled and quartered

¾ cup (185 mL) buttermilk

2 Tbsp (30 mL) butter, melted

Salt and white pepper to taste

3½ oz (100 g) Roquefort cheese, pulled into tiny nuggets

2 Tbsp (30 mL) snipped fresh chives

preparation time	● 10 minutes
cooking time	● 18–20 minu·
makes	● 6 servings

ERIC'S OPTIONS
Instead of Roquefort, try any other creamy blue cheese in this recipe. For golden-hued potatoes, use Yukon Gold potatoes instead of russets or baking potatoes. If you can't find chives, mix 2 thinly sliced green onions into the mashed potatoes.

Place the potatoes in a pot, cover with cold water by at least 2 inches (5 cm) and bring to a boil over medium-high heat. Reduce the heat until the potatoes simmer gently. Simmer until very tender, 18 to 20 minutes.

Drain the potatoes well, then mash thoroughly. Mix in the buttermilk and butter until well combined and season with salt and pepper. Mix in the cheese and chives and serve.

TIPS FOR MAKING MASHED POTATOES

If you want to make smooth, light, lump-free mashed potatoes, use a floury potato, such as a russet or baking potato. These types of potatoes have a high starch level that allows you to mash them vigorously until lump-free without worrying about them turning gummy and sticky.

Yukon Gold or yellow-fleshed potatoes have a medium starch level that yields a denser, slightly moister, yet still delicious, mashed potato. Waxy, low-starch potatoes, such as smooth-skinned red or white potatoes, turn unappealingly gummy if overly mashed. You can still mash them, but it's best to get them only just smooth or still a little coarse in texture. I often boil and mash these types of potatoes with the skin on.

When preparing the potatoes for cooking, cut them into evenly sized quarters, or even halves, depending on their size. If you cut the potatoes too small, they can become waterlogged and, when cooked, will taste more like water than potato. If you cut the potatoes unevenly, the smaller pieces will overcook and fall apart while you wait for larger pieces to cook.

Cook the potatoes in a generous amount of cold water. I usually cover them with at least 2 inches (5 cm) of cold water. If you don't use a generous amount of water, starch leaching from the potatoes as they cook can concentrate and give the potatoes a gluey texture. Simmer the potatoes gently. If you boil them rapidly they'll cook too quickly and start to fall apart on the outside before the center is done.

When the potatoes are very tender, drain them well. If the potatoes seem overly moist, set the pot back on the heat to dry for a minute or so. To avoid lumps, be sure to mash them when they are piping hot. If they cool for too long, they won't mash as well. Add any ingredients such as butter and milk after the potatoes have been mashed. If you add them before, particularly if the ingredients are not warm, they can cool the potatoes down and cause them to lump, no matter how vigorously you mash them afterward.

WHIPPED YUKON GOLD POTATOES

These light and airy potatoes seem to fly off the plate they taste so good, particularly when served with anything savory and saucy, such as Pork Chops in Sumptuous Three-Mushroom Sauce (page 104).

2½ lb (1.25 kg) Yukon Gold potatoes, peeled, quartered and rinsed well

½ cup (125 mL) warm milk

3 Tbsp (45 mL) melted butter

Salt and white pepper to taste

Place the potatoes in a pot, cover with cold water by at least 2 inches (5 cm) and bring to a boil over medium-high heat. Reduce the heat until the potatoes simmer gently. Simmer until very tender, 18 to 20 minutes.

Drain the potatoes well and mash thoroughly. Add the milk, butter and salt and pepper. Beat the potatoes with a handheld mixer until the potatoes are light and airy, then serve.

preparation time	•	5 minutes
cooking time	•	18–20 minu
makes	•	6 servings

ERIC'S OPTIONS
The potatoes could also be whipped in a standmixer. To do so, place the well-drained, cooked potatoes in the mixer bowl. Fit the mixer with its paddle attachment and beat the potatoes until smooth. Replace the paddle attachment with the whipping attachment. Add the milk, butter and salt and pepper and whip the potatoes until light and airy.

BOILED, SMASHED and FRIED NEW POTATOES

This recipe (pictured on page 102) provides a three-step method for cooking miniature new potatoes that makes them tender in the middle and deliciously crispy on the outside: a very good thing!

preparation time	• 5 minutes
cooking time	• 14–16 minutes
makes	• 4 servings

8 miniature red-skinned potatoes

8 miniature white-skinned potatoes

4 Tbsp (60 mL) olive oil

Salt and freshly ground black pepper to taste

2 tsp (10 mL) chopped fresh rosemary

ERIC'S OPTIONS
For added flavor and color, lightly sprinkle the potatoes with pinches of ground cumin and paprika while they fry.

Place potatoes in a pot and cover with cold water. Gently boil them until they are just tender and still holding their shape, about 10 minutes. Drain well, set in a single layer on a baking sheet and let cool until the potatoes are safe to handle, but still warm. Place a potato on a clean work surface and, with the palm of your hand, gently press it into a thick disk. Set the potato back on the baking sheet. Repeat with the remaining potatoes.

Preheat the oven to 200°F (95°C).

Pour 2 Tbsp (30 mL) of the oil into a large skillet and set over medium-high heat. Add half the potatoes. Season with salt and pepper and sprinkle with 1 tsp (5 mL) of the rosemary. Cook the potatoes for 2 to 3 minutes per side, or until golden and crispy. Transfer to a serving platter and keep warm in the oven. Repeat with the remaining potatoes, and then serve.

CRISPY OVEN FRIES

These potatoes (pictured on page 112) don't last long around my house. They're crispy on the outside and fluffy in the middle, and they taste sublime sprinkled with malt vinegar or dunked into ketchup.

preparation time • 10 minutes
cooking time • 25 minutes
makes • 4–6 serving

3 Tbsp (45 mL) vegetable oil

1 tsp (5 mL) coarse sea salt, or to taste

1 tsp (5 mL) coarsely ground black pepper, or to taste

½ tsp (2.5 mL) sweet paprika (see About Paprika on page 71)

3 large baking potatoes

ERIC'S OPTIONS
Instead of using salt, pepper and paprika, season the potatoes to taste with your favorite brand of seasoning salt.

Place an oven rack in the middle position. Preheat the oven to 450°F (230°C).

Combine the oil, salt, pepper and paprika in a large bowl. Cut each potato in half lengthwise, then cut each half into 6 lengthwise wedges. Place the potatoes in the bowl and toss to coat. Arrange the potatoes in a single layer on a large nonstick baking sheet. Bake for 20 minutes, or until the potatoes are tender in the center and crisp on the bottom. Turn the oven to broil and cook the potatoes until golden and crispy on top, about 5 minutes. (Broiling eliminates the time-consuming step of trying to flip each potato individually and roasting them until brown on the other side.) Keep an eye on them as they broil so that they don't overbrown.

ROASTED POTATOES with HONEY, DIJON and PEPPER

Honey and mustard always go well together, whether in a dipping sauce for chicken or, in this case, a glaze for roasted potatoes. When roasted, these potatoes are sticky, sweet, peppery, crisply coated and yummy!

preparation time • 10 minutes
cooking time • 40–45 minutes
makes • 4–6 servings

3 Tbsp (45 mL) olive oil

2 Tbsp (30 mL) honey

2 Tbsp (30 mL) whole grain Dijon mustard

2 Tbsp (30 mL) fresh lemon juice

1 tsp (5 mL) coarsely ground black pepper

½ tsp (2.5 mL) salt

6 medium red- or white-skinned potatoes, cut into 1-inch (2.5 cm) cubes

2 green onions, thinly sliced

ERIC'S OPTIONS
For a smoother texture, use regular Dijon mustard instead of whole grain. Instead of cubing medium red or white new potatoes, cut 20 to 24 miniature red- or white-skinned new potatoes in half and toss and roast them in the honey and Dijon mixture.

Preheat the oven to 375°F (190°C). Line a baking sheet with parchment paper.

Place the oil, honey, mustard, lemon juice, pepper and salt in a large bowl and whisk to combine. Add the potatoes and toss to coat. Spread the potatoes in a single layer on the prepared baking sheet. Roast for 40 to 45 minutes, turning occasionally, until they are golden brown and tender. Spoon the potatoes into a serving dish, sprinkle with green onion and serve.

BROCCOLI and CHEDDAR–STUFFED POTATOES

This is probably the fussiest side dish in this book. You have to bake the potatoes, cool them a bit, remove the flesh, mash it, mix it with the flavorings, stuff the mixture back into the potato shells and bake them again. After one bite of these cheesy, broccoli-flecked spuds, though, I'm always glad I made the effort.

4 medium baking potatoes, washed and dried

5 oz (150 g) piece broccoli crown, cut into 6 florets (see Note)

¼ cup (60 mL) milk

2 Tbsp (30 mL) melted butter

2 Tbsp (30 mL) sour cream

3½ oz (100 g) cheddar cheese, grated

2 green onions, thinly sliced

Salt and white pepper to taste

preparation time	•	30 minutes
cooking time	•	90 minutes
makes	•	4 servings

NOTE
A broccoli crown is the top portion of the vegetable with the stem removed.

ERIC'S OPTIONS
Asparagus is a delicious substitute for broccoli in the stuffed potatoes. Snap off and discard the tough stem-end of 8 asparagus spears. Thinly slice the spears and cook in boiling water for 30 seconds. Cool in cold water, drain well and mix into the potatoes when asked to add the broccoli in the method.

Preheat the oven to 375°F (190°C).

Prick each potato a few times with a fork. Bake for 65 minutes, or until quite tender. While the potatoes bake, cook the broccoli in boiling water for 2 minutes. Cool in ice-cold water, drain well and chop coarsely.

When the potatoes are done, leave the oven on. Let the potatoes cool until safe enough to handle but still quite warm. Cut off the top third of each potato. Carefully scoop out as much potato flesh as you can from the top and bottom pieces of potato and place it in a bowl. Discard the top pieces of potato skin; place the bottom, hollowed-out potato shells in a baking dish. Mash the potato flesh until smooth, then beat in the milk, butter and sour cream. Mix in the broccoli, three-quarters of the cheese, and the green onions, salt and pepper.

Pack and mound the mixture into the potato shells and sprinkle the remaining cheese overtop. Bake for 25 minutes, or until golden brown.

BOILED MINI POTATOES with GRAINY MUSTARD and LEMON

Simply boiled potatoes are given a splendid, tangy taste by tossing them with mustard and fresh lemon juice.

preparation time	•	5 minutes
cooking time	•	10–12 minutes
makes	•	6 servings

24–30 miniature red- or white-skinned potatoes, washed well

2 green onions, thinly sliced

2 Tbsp (30 mL) whole grain Dijon mustard, or to taste

2 Tbsp (30 mL) extra virgin olive oil, or to taste

1 Tbsp (15 mL) fresh lemon juice, or to taste

Salt and freshly ground black pepper to taste

ERIC'S OPTIONS
Instead of using green onion, toss the potatoes with a chopped or snipped fresh herb to taste, such as parsley, dill, tarragon or chives.

Place the potatoes in a pot and cover with cold water. Gently boil the potatoes until just tender, 10 to 12 minutes. Drain well and place in a serving bowl. Toss in the remaining ingredients and serve the potatoes hot or at room temperature.

Read "About Green Onions and Scallions" on the next page . . .

ABOUT GREEN ONIONS AND SCALLIONS

Although these two vegetables can be used interchangeably in recipes, and taste and look similar, they are different members of the onion family.

A green onion is any immature onion, whether the bulb is yellow, white or red, with greens still attached. The bulb on a green onion can range from almost nonexistent to quite large. Those with white and almost nonexistent bulbs are what you'll see for sale at most supermarkets. Those with larger and differently colored bulbs, such as red, can often be seen for sale at farmers' markets.

Scallions are also known as spring onions. This vegetable is a special variety of white onion that does not form an enlarged bulb and that can be identified by its straight sides at the root end.

GINGER MASHED SQUASH

This recipe (pictured on page 135) calls for the oblong-shaped banana squash, which has a golden-orange, fine-textured flesh. It's also a very large variety of squash, growing 2 feet (60 cm) or more in length. Because of that, most supermarkets cut this squash into chunks that are cleaned, meaning the seeds are removed.

2 lb (1 kg) cleaned banana squash, peeled and cubed

2 Tbsp (30 mL) peeled, chopped fresh ginger (see About Fresh Ginger on page 30)

2 garlic cloves, thinly sliced

2 Tbsp (30 mL) butter

2 green onions, thinly sliced

Salt and freshly ground black pepper to taste

preparation time •	10 minutes
cooking time •	10–12 minutes
makes •	4 servings

ERIC'S OPTIONS

Try 2 lb (1 kg) of another cleaned squash in this recipe, such as butternut. If you like the pungent taste of cilantro, mix 2 Tbsp (30 mL) of chopped fresh cilantro into the mashed squash instead of green onion.

Place the squash, ginger and garlic in a pot and cover with cold water. Bring to a boil over medium-high heat. Reduce the heat until the water gently simmers. Simmer the squash until very tender, 10 to 12 minutes. Drain the squash well and set back over the heat to evaporate any excess water. Remove from the heat and mash thoroughly. Mix in the butter, green onion and salt and pepper.

BROCCOLI with LEMON ZEST, GINGER and RED PEPPER

Broccoli turns a brilliant green color when boiled until just tender. In this recipe (pictured on page 73), that stunning color is tastily accented with hints of yellow from lemon zest and flashes of stop-sign red from the bell pepper.

preparation time	•	10 minutes
cooking time	•	5–7 minutes
makes	•	4–6 servings

ERIC'S OPTIONS
If you're a fan of garlic, add a minced clove when cooking the red pepper.

2 Tbsp (30 mL) butter

½ medium red bell pepper, finely diced

1–2 tsp (5–10 mL) peeled, finely chopped fresh ginger (see About Fresh Ginger on page 30)

½ **cup (125 mL)** chicken stock

18 medium-sized broccoli florets

1 tsp (5 mL) finely grated lemon zest

Salt and freshly ground black pepper to taste

Bring a large pot of water to a boil. Meanwhile, place the butter in a large skillet and set over medium heat. When the butter is melted, add the red pepper and ginger and cook until the pepper is tender, 3 to 4 minutes. Add the stock and bring to a simmer. Reduce the heat to medium-low.

When the water is boiling, add the broccoli and cook until just tender, 2 to 3 minutes. Drain well and add the broccoli to the skillet. Sprinkle in the lemon zest and salt and pepper, toss to combine and serve.

ABOUT BELL PEPPERS

Bell peppers are named for their bell-like shape. When young, most are green in color, with a slightly sharp taste. As they mature and ripen on the vine they sweeten in flavor, become more thickly fleshed, and, depending on the variety, change from green to another color, such as yellow, orange or red.

Look for firm bell peppers with a deep color and a glossy sheen that feel heavy for their size. Store them in a plastic bag in the refrigerator for up to a week.

Bell peppers are an excellent source of vitamin C, and also contain vitamin A and a variety of other nutrients.

GREEN BEANS with PECANS, LIME and HONEY

These quick-cooking beans (pictured on page 140) are sweetened with honey, made tangy with lime juice and enriched with the buttery taste of pecans.

3 Tbsp (45 mL) honey

2 Tbsp (30 mL) fresh lime juice

1 lb (500 g) green beans, trimmed

⅓ cup (80 mL) pecan halves, coarsely chopped

Salt and freshly ground black pepper to taste

preparation time • 6 minutes
cooking time • 5 minutes
makes • 4 servings

ERIC'S OPTIONS
For a green and yellow color and two-bean taste, replace ½ lb (250 g) of the green beans with wax (yellow) beans.

Bring a large pot of water to a boil to cook the beans. Meanwhile, warm the honey and lime juice in a large skillet set over low heat.

When the water is boiling, add the beans and cook until they are a vibrant green and just tender, 2 to 3 minutes. Drain the beans well, then add them with the pecans and salt and pepper to the skillet, toss to combine and serve.

CANDIED CARROTS and PARSNIPS with PEAS

Earthy-tasting root vegetables are simmered and glazed in butter, brown sugar, citrus juice and spice in this recipe (pictured on page 101). This makes a nice side dish for many of the meat dishes in this book, such as Boneless Pork Chops with Apples, Onion and Sage (page 100).

preparation time	•	10 minutes
cooking time	•	8–10 minutes
makes	•	6 servings

ERIC'S OPTIONS
If you want to cook only one type of root vegetable, use double the volume of the root vegetable of your choice and omit the other one.

2 medium carrots, peeled, halved lengthwise and sliced

2 medium parsnips, peeled, halved lengthwise and sliced

2 Tbsp (30 mL) butter

2 Tbsp (30 mL) golden brown sugar

2 Tbsp (30 mL) orange juice

2 tsp (10 mL) fresh lemon juice

¼ tsp (1 mL) ground cinnamon

⅛ tsp (0.5 mL) ground nutmeg

Salt and freshly ground black pepper to taste

¾ cup (185 mL) frozen peas

Place the carrots and parsnips in a pot and cover with cold water. Gently boil the vegetables until just tender, 5 minutes, then drain well. Place the butter in a large skillet or wide pot and set over medium heat. When the butter is melted, add the brown sugar, orange juice, lemon juice, cinnamon and nutmeg and cook, stirring, until the brown sugar is melted. Add the carrots and parsnips and cook, stirring, for 2 to 3 minutes, or until nicely glazed with the butter/sugar/juice mixture. Sprinkle in the peas and heat them through for 1 to 2 minutes. Season with salt and pepper, and serve.

MIXED VEGETABLE STIR-FRY
in SWEET CHILI SAUCE

Be sure to have all the elements of this quick-cooking stir-fry chopped and/or measured before you fire up your wok or skillet. This colorful side dish is, of course, great to serve alongside Asian-style dishes, such as Hoisin Chili Beef Back Ribs (pictured; recipe page 132).

1 Tbsp (15 mL) vegetable oil

1 small onion, halved and sliced

1 medium red bell pepper, cubed

1 medium carrot, halved lengthwise and thinly sliced

18 snow peas, tips trimmed

2 baby bok choy, washed, separated into leaves and coarsely chopped (see About Bok Choy on page 37)

2 green onions cut into 1-inch (2.5 cm) pieces

1 garlic clove, minced

1–2 tsp (5–10 mL) peeled, finely chopped fresh ginger (see About Fresh Ginger on page 30)

⅓ cup (80 mL) Thai-style sweet chili sauce (see Note)

2 Tbsp (30 mL) water

preparation time	• 15 minutes
cooking time	• 5 minutes
makes	• 6 servings

NOTE
Thai-style sweet chili sauce is available at Asian food stores and in the Asian foods aisle of most supermarkets.

ERIC'S OPTIONS
If you like bean sprouts, mix 1 cup (250 mL) of them into this stir-fry at the end of cooking. Heat through for about 30 seconds before serving.

Place the oil in a wok or large skillet and set over medium-high heat. When very hot, add the onion, bell pepper and carrot and stir-fry for 2 minutes. Add the snow peas, bok choy, green onions, garlic and ginger and stir-fry for 1 minute more. Mix in the sweet chili sauce and water and bring to a simmer. Stir-fry until the vegetables are nicely glazed with sauce, about 1 minute, then serve.

BRUSSELS SPROUTS with APPLES and WALNUTS

In this recipe, the sometimes intense taste of Brussels sprouts is sweetly tempered by simmering and glazing them in apple juice.

1 lb (500 g) Brussels sprouts, each about 1 inch (2.5 cm) round, trimmed

¾ cup (185 mL) apple juice

1 small red apple, cored and finely diced

2 tsp (10 mL) fresh lemon juice

¼ cup (60 mL) walnut pieces

1 Tbsp (15 mL) butter

Salt and pepper to taste

preparation time • 10 minutes
cooking time • 8 minutes
makes • 4 servings

ERIC'S OPTIONS
Instead of walnuts, use pecan pieces. For another taste element, mix 1 tsp (5 mL) of finely chopped ginger into the apple juice mixture when bringing to a boil.

Bring a large pot of water to a boil. Boil the Brussels sprouts for 4 minutes, or until firm/tender (according to preference), then drain well. Cool the sprouts in ice-cold water and drain well again. Place the apple juice, diced apple and lemon juice in a wide skillet and bring to a boil. Add the Brussels sprouts and reduce the heat to a simmer. Cook until the Brussels sprouts are heated through and tender and the apple juice is almost reduced to a glaze. Mix in the nuts, butter and salt and pepper. Spoon into a dish and serve.

INDEX

ABOUT THE AUTHOR

Eric Akis has been food writer for the *Victoria Times Colonist* since 1997. His biweekly recipe-rich columns are published in newspapers across Canada. Prior to becoming a journalist, Akis trained as a professional chef and pastry chef. He worked for 15 years in a variety of operations in Ontario and British Columbia, from fine hotels to restaurants to catering companies.

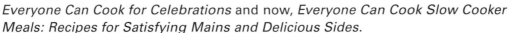
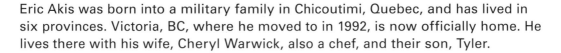

In 2003, his experiences as a chef and food writer inspired him to create the bestselling Everyone Can Cook series of cookbooks, which includes *Everyone Can Cook, Everyone Can Cook Seafood, Everyone Can Cook Appetizers, Everyone Can Cook Midweek Meals, Everyone Can Cook for Celebrations* and now, *Everyone Can Cook Slow Cooker Meals: Recipes for Satisfying Mains and Delicious Sides.*

Eric Akis was born into a military family in Chicoutimi, Quebec, and has lived in six provinces. Victoria, BC, where he moved to in 1992, is now officially home. He lives there with his wife, Cheryl Warwick, also a chef, and their son, Tyler.

To learn more about Eric Akis and his books, visit www.everyonecancook.com.